From Your Friends At **The MAILBOX**®

JUNE

A MONTH OF IDEAS AT YOUR FINGERTIPS!

PRESCHOOL–KINDERGARTEN

WRITTEN BY
Barbara Backer, Diane Gilliam, Ada Goren, Lucia Kemp Henry,
Lori Kent, Angie Kutzer, Lisa Leonardi, Suzanne Moore,
Vicki Mockaitis Pacchetti, Mackie Rhodes, Dayle Timmons

EDITED BY
Lynn Bemer Coble, Jayne Gammons, Ada Goren,
Jennifer Rudisill, Debbie Shoffner, Gina Sutphin

ILLUSTRATED BY
Jennifer Bennett, Cathy Spangler Bruce, Pam Crane, Clevell Harris,
Lucia Kemp Henry, Susan Hodnett, Sheila Krill, Mary Lester, Rob
Mayworth, Rebecca Saunders, Barry Slate, Donna K. Teal

TYPESET BY
Scott Lyons, Lynette Maxwell

COVER DESIGNED BY
Jennifer Bennett

Visit our Web site at www.themailbox.com.

©1997 by THE EDUCATION CENTER, INC.
All rights reserved.
ISBN# 1-56234-189-8

Manufactured in the United States

10 9 8 7 6 5 4 3

TABLE OF CONTENTS

I took
a walk
today!

June Calendar

National Fresh Fruit And Vegetable Month

Celebrate the abundance, variety, and nutritional value of fruits and vegetables this month. Throughout the month, discuss the importance fruits and vegetables have in keeping our bodies healthy—such as providing vitamins, giving us energy, and helping us to grow. Then taste-test several different kinds of fruits and vegetables, and compile a group graph of your student's favorites.

National Skin Safety Month

Summer is the time we start thinking about fun in the sun. It is also the perfect time to discuss with your students the importance of protecting our skins from the sun's damaging rays. Throughout the month, demonstrate ways to protect skin from the sun, such as wearing sunscreen, hats, visors, and sunglasses. Also discuss the importance of drinking lots of water to keep skin from dehydrating. Then prepare for a Fun In The Sun Day. On a chosen day, invite your students to wear hats and sunglasses to school. Slather up each child with sunscreen; then head outside for some group games.

Pet Appreciation Week (June 6–12)

From poodles to parrots, pets enrich our lives in many ways. Invite your students to demonstrate their pet appreciation by bringing their animals to school for a visit. Enlist the help of parents to schedule times during the week for family pets to visit school. If a child doesn't have a pet, encourage him to bring a stuffed pet or a picture of a pet he would like to have. Invite students to share the things they appreciate about their pets. At the end of the week, prepare a pet appreciation book. Have each student draw a picture of his pet; then write down his words as he completes the sentence "I appreciate my pet because_____." Compile all the pages into a class book. What a "purr-fect" way to show pet appreciation!

National Hug Holiday Week (Second Week In June)

Embrace this special holiday by teaching your youngsters the song "Four Hugs A Day" (*10 Carrot Diamond;* Charlotte Diamond Music). Hold hands to form a group circle while singing the song. Then, at the end of the song, start a hand-hug. Squeeze the hand of the child standing next to you; then, as his hand is squeezed, he in turn squeezes the hand of the child standing next to him. Continue the hand-hug around the circle in the same manner until it returns to the person who started it. Hooray for hugs! (For more information contact Hugs for Health Foundation, P.O. Box 1704, Tustin, CA 92781.)

Donut Day (First Friday In June)

Donut Day was begun in Chicago in 1938 by the Salvation Army as a fund-raising campaign during the Great Depression. Donut Day is now an annual tradition. Celebrate this tasty day by preparing and eating donuts with your students. To make a donut, cut a hole in the center of a refrigerated biscuit using the plastic lid of a soda bottle. Fry the biscuit in hot oil until it is golden brown and puffy. When the donut is slightly cool, place it in a bag. Add some cinnamon and sugar; then shake, shake, shake. Yummy!

5—Richard Scarry's Birthday

Born on June 5, 1919, Richard Scarry is the author and illustrator of more than 250 children's books. Read aloud his classic *Busy Town* (Western Publishing Company, Inc.); then invite students to work in cooperative groups to create their own busy towns. Provide each group with a sheet of heavy cardboard or poster board on which to build a town using recyclable materials such as boxes, egg cartons, cans, and containers. Encourage students to draw animal figures and display them in their town. Display the towns side by side in your classroom and invite youngsters and classroom visitors to take a Busy Town Tour!

18—First American Woman In Space Anniversary

On June 18, 1983, Dr. Sally Ride became the first American woman in space. She served as a mission specialist on a six-day mission aboard the space shuttle *Challenger*. Invite students to share their knowledge about space travel and astronauts. Then ask the question, "Would you like to be an astronaut?" Have students graph their responses on a sheet of bulletin-board paper cut into a rocket shape.

24—Celebration Of The Senses Day

Stimulate your little ones' senses today by whipping up a batch of peanut-butter play dough. Have youngsters prepare individual portions by mixing together equal quantities of peanut butter and nonfat dried milk. Add some honey if desired; then knead until smooth. As a child manipulates the dough, he will use his senses of touch, sight, smell, and sound. And when he is done sculpting with the dough he may taste it, too!

27—Happy Birthday To "Happy Birthday To You"

On this day in 1859, Mildred J. Hill, a schoolteacher from Louisville, Kentucky, wrote the melody for "Happy Birthday To You." Each minute, somewhere around the globe, this song is being sung, making it the most popular song in the world. Celebrate this special day by hosting a birthday party for the birthday song. Play musical chairs using the birthday song for music; then end your mini-celebration with a round of "Happy Birthday To You" and birthday cupcakes!

June

CLASSROOM NEWS

Teacher: _____ Date: _____

A Peek At The Week

Looking Ahead

Reminders

Help Wanted

Special Thanks

Let The

Take a walk on the sunny side of the curriculum with this hot collection of dazzling activities that are sure to warm the hearts of your little sunseekers!

by Lori Kent

Sing A Song Of Sunshine

Sing this sunny tune to help young-sters understand the many benefits of our spectacular star.

(sung to the tune of "When Johnny Comes Marching Home")

The sun is shining in the sky—a star—so bright.
It shines down on the earth and gives us
 warmth and light.
The sun helps plants and flowers grow.
It gives us clouds and bright rainbows.
Oh, the sun is shining high, in the sky.
What a beautiful sight!

A Time To Shine

Spread some sunshine throughout your classroom in preparation for this dazzling unit. Hang yellow and or-ange crepe-paper streamers and lengths of metallic rib-bon from the ceiling of your room to give the feel of spar-kling sunshine. Next use yellow tape to make a sun shape on your floor, making as many sun rays as there are children in your classroom. Sprinkle a path of gold plastic confetti (available at party-supply stores) from the door of your classroom to the sun on the floor. On the first morning of your unit, play some lively tropical music in the background; then greet your little ones at your classroom door wearing a wide-brimmed hat and sun-glasses. Invite each child to follow the confetti path, then sit on a sun ray. What a sunny way to start the unit!

Warm-Up

Now that students are shining with anticipation, introduce your sunshine unit with a brainstorming session. In ad-vance, cut a large circle from yellow bul-letin-board paper; then cut several strips from orange bulletin-board paper. Read aloud *Sun Up, Sun Down* by Gail Gib-bons (Harcourt Brace Jovanovich, Pub-lishers). Afterward have your little ones recall some facts about the sun; then print each fact on an orange strip. Dis-play the strips around the yellow circle on a wall in your classroom for refer-ence during the remainder of your unit.

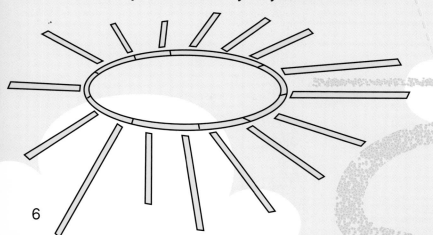

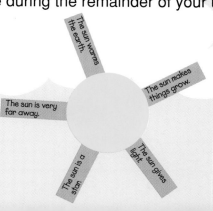

Sun Shine!

Warm Up And Melt Down

Your youngsters will be powered up on solar science after participating in this experiment that demonstrates the sun's warmth. Provide each child with a few spoonfuls of chocolate chips inside a resealable plastic bag. Instruct each child to place his bag near a sunny window or outside in a sunny spot. Have students check the bags every ten minutes. Ask volunteers to guess why the chips melted. Write their comments on a sheet of chart paper. Lead students to the conclusion that the heat from the sun melted the chocolate chips. Save the bags of melted chips to make Peanut Butter Power Bars as a tasty follow-up to this activity.

Peanut Butter Power Bars

Put the information your little ones have learned about the sun's heat to yummy use with this solar-powered snack. To make one power bar, have a child spread a thin layer of peanut butter onto a graham cracker; then cut a corner from the bottom of a bag of melted chips (see "Warm Up And Melt Down"). Instruct her to gently squeeze the bag of melted chips, drizzling the chocolate over the peanut butter. Serve the Peanut Butter Power Bar with a cup of milk. Yum-yum-yummy!

Sunshiny Faces

Create a sparkling display of sunshiny faces with this bright idea. Duplicate a class supply of the sun pattern (page 12) onto yellow construction paper; then cut out all the suns. Have each youngster paint a cutout using a mixture of thinned yellow-colored glue to which clear glitter has been added. Have her cover the outside edges of the sun cutout with orange-colored glue, then sprinkle on clear glitter. When the glue has thoroughly dried, cut out the center of each sun as indicated. Tape a photo of each child to the underside of her sun, so that her picture is framed within the circle. Display your little sunshines on a bulletin board with the title "Spectacular Stars!"

7

Colorful Light

After participating in these outdoor centers, your little ones will discover that a little ray of sunshine contains all the colors of the rainbow.

Prism Center

Spread a white sheet on the ground; then challenge students to use prisms to see the sun's rainbow of light reflected onto the sheet.

Bubble Center

Mix up a batch of bubble solution by combining 1 3/4 cups of dishwashing liquid and 14 cups of water in a large tub or bucket. Add a collection of bubble blowers. Then, as a child blows a bubble, encourage him to notice the rainbow of colors on each bubble as the sun shines through the bubble solution.

Water Zone

Invite students to pour water from watering cans, or spray water with a garden hose. Remind them to look for the rainbows caused by the sun's light shining through the water droplets.

Shine On Me!

Provide youngsters with a firsthand opportunity to see the sun in action. On a sunny day, plan to take your students for an outdoor walk around your school. During the walk, encourage your little sunseekers to notice things that the sun shines on; then return to your classroom to make these individual booklets. Duplicate a supply of the booklet pages from page 13; then cut them apart. Invite each student to illustrate as many pages as she wishes, showing things that the sun shines on. Then write her completion to the sentence "Sunshine on _____," on each page. Encourage her to illustrate a final page showing the sun shining on herself. Complete its sentence to read "Sunshine on [Child's name]." Staple the pages together between construction-paper covers.

Sun Prints

Your little ones will delight in this project that uses the sun's light to create interesting prints. In advance, gather some small items, such as keys, feathers, leaves, necklaces, doilies, combs, forks, and seeds. To make a print, lay a sheet of blue construction paper outside in bright sunlight. Place a variety of objects on the paper. Leave the paper in the sun for several hours; then remove the objects. Your youngsters will be amazed to see images of the objects that the sunlight could not shine through.

Sunny Centers

Let the sun shine into your center activities with these ideas.

Art Center

Watch your students' interests soar when you enhance your art center with some of the supplies listed below.

- yellow and orange paint to which gold glitter has been added
- yellow, orange, and red crepe and tissue paper
- yellow, orange, and red colored glue
- yellow, orange, and red construction paper
- gold, silver, and clear glitter
- strips of Mylar® or metallic ribbon
- paper plates

Block Center

Place a floor lamp or clamp a utility lamp to a shelf in your block area so that children can experiment with making shadows. Before opening the center, discuss safety precautions with your youngsters regarding the use of the lamp. (As always, supervision is the best precaution.)

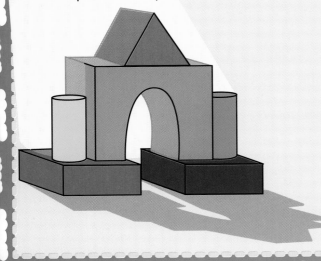

Music Center

Add a little razzle-dazzle to your music center with these terrific tambourines. To make one, paint the bottom of a paper plate yellow and allow it to dry. Fold the plate in half; then glue lengths of yellow and orange crepe paper to the inside rim of half the plate. Add several spoonfuls of dried beans to the inside of the folded plate; then staple the edges together. Invite youngsters to shake their tambourines while listening to a few of the sunny songs listed below.

"Sunshine Medley"
Sung by Greg and Steve
Rockin' Down The Road; Youngheart Music, Inc.

"Get Up & Get Going/This Land Is Your Land"
Sung by Anna Moo
Making Moosic; Music For Little People

"May There Always Be Sunshine"
Sung by Charlotte Diamond
10 Carrot Diamond; Hug Bug Records

Play-Dough Center

Add a little solar shine to your play-dough center with this sparkling recipe.

Sparkling Play Dough

1 cup all-purpose flour
1/2 cup salt
1 cup water
1 Tbsp. cream of tartar

1 Tbsp. vegetable oil
yellow food coloring
lemon extract
clear glitter

Mix the flour, salt, water, cream of tartar, and vegetable oil with the desired amount of food coloring and lemon extract in a pan. Place the pan over low heat and stir until the mixture forms a ball that pulls away from the sides of the pan. Remove the pan from the heat, and place the dough on a flat surface. Knead in as much glitter as desired. Continue kneading until the dough is smooth and pliable. Store in an airtight container.

Math Center

Your little ones will be catching more than rays at this math center that focuses on patterning and number skills. On the floor or on a tabletop in your math area, use masking tape to make a sun design. Vary the length of each ray. Challenge each student to use a set of math counters to create a pattern along a sun ray. Extend this activity by asking each child to count the number of manipulatives she placed along each ray. What a sunny center!

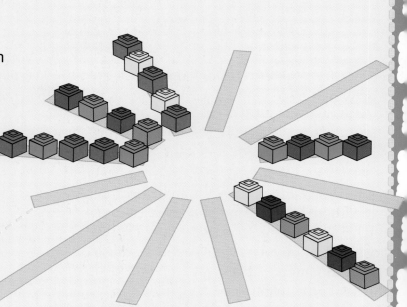

Reading Center

Heat up your reading center with these sizzling stories.

When The Sun Rose
Written by Barbara Helen Berger
Published by Philomel Books

Sun Song
Written by Jean Marzollo
Published by HarperCollins Publishers, Inc.

Sunshine Celebration

Your little ones will be ablaze with sunny attire after making these suits and souvenirs to culminate your sunshine unit!

Sunbeam T's

Top off your sunshine unit by making these cool sunbeam shirts. Send home copies of the parent letter on page 15 requesting that each child bring a clean, white T-shirt to school. Assist each child in pulling up sections of his T-shirt, then twisting a rubber band around each section. Dye each shirt yellow according to the package directions on a box of Rit® Dye. When each shirt is thoroughly dry, remove the rubber bands to reveal bright, yellow sunbursts. Groovy!

Sunny Visors

Your youngsters will be ready for lots of fun in the sun when they team up these nifty visors with sunbeam shirts (see "Sunbeam T's"). For each child, trace a sun visor pattern (page 14) onto tagboard; then cut it out. Invite a student to decorate his visor using his choice of art materials. Punch a hole in each end of the visor. Thread a length of string elastic through each hole and tie them in place. Tie the lengths of elastic together to provide a snug fit. Your little ones will be proud to wear their sunny suits for all to see.

Sunshine Souvenir

Mark the end of your sunshine unit by providing each student with a sunshine souvenir. Duplicate a class supply of the award on page 15 onto yellow construction paper. Take a photo of each child wearing his sunbeam T-shirt and sun visor. Program an award for each child; then attach his picture. Present him with his award on the last day of your unit. What a sunny delight!

Souvenir Of A Sunny Unit

Name _Mark Kidney_
Date _June 17, 1998_

Sun Pattern
Use with "Sunshiny Faces" on page 7.

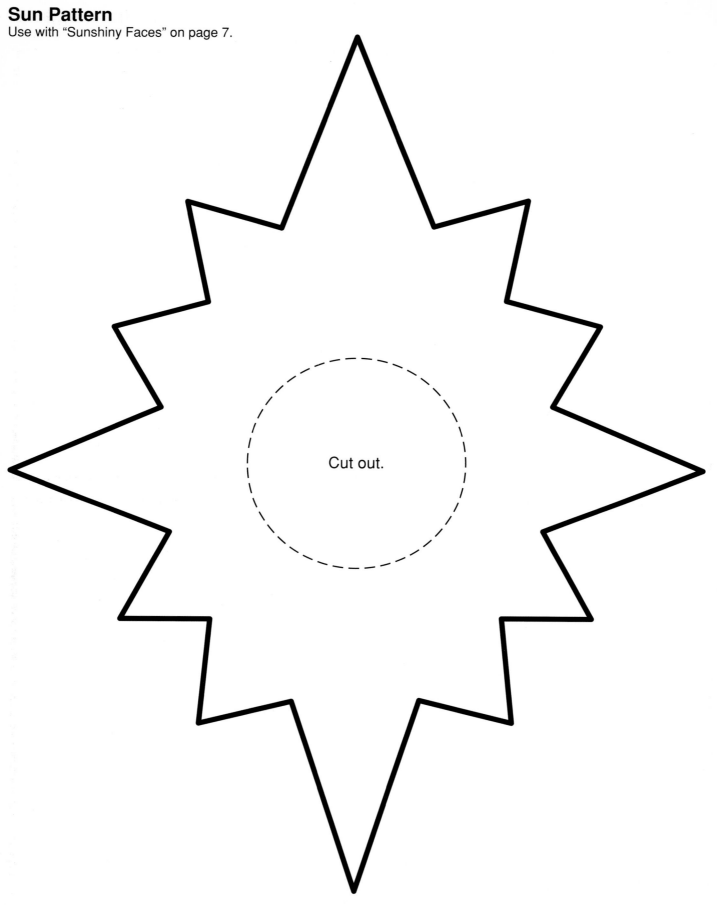

Cut out.

Sunshine on _____ .

Sunshine on _____ .

Visor Pattern
Use with "Sunny Visors" on page 11.

Dear Family,

To commemorate our sunshine unit, we will be making sunburst T-shirts. You can help us by sending a clean, white T-shirt to school. Please label the inside of the shirt with your little sunseeker's name. At school each child will have an opportunity to tie-dye his/her shirt yellow. Don't be surprised if your child comes home beaming with pride over a "sun-sational" shirt!

Please send a T-shirt to school by _____.

(date)

Thanks so much for your help!

©1997 The Education Center, Inc. • *JUNE* • TEC756

Souvenir Of A Sunny Unit

Place photo here.

Name _____

Date _____

©1997 The Education Center, Inc. • *JUNE* • TEC756

Let's Go Outside!

The weather is warm and the sun is shining, so head outdoors for some fun with hoops, boxes, chalk, streamers, bubbles, and more!

ideas contributed by dayle timmons

Takin' A Walk

Scavenger Hunt

Help little ones get to know the great outdoors with a scavenger hunt for natural objects. In advance, walk through your play yard, into a nearby wooded area, or down a neighborhood street close to your classroom. Take note of what items could be collected, such as leaves, sticks, rocks, wildflowers, or pinecones. Then prepare a picture list of these items, similar to the one shown. Keep it simple by asking youngsters to find only one of each object, or add numerals to spark some counting practice.

On the day of your hunt, give each child a copy of the picture list and a paper lunch bag. Then set out together to find the listed objects. Upon returning to your classroom, invite little ones to form small groups and show off their natural treasures. They'll have fun "checking" one another's lists to make sure they found everything.

For The Birds

Take along pairs of makeshift binoculars on your next walk, and encourage youngsters to do a little bird-watching. To prepare, give each child two empty toilet-tissue tubes. Invite each child to decorate his tubes with crayons or stickers. Then use masking tape to attach the two rolls side by side to resemble a pair of binoculars. Next share pictures or photographs of birds from a good nonfiction book, such as *About Birds: A Guide For Children* by Cathryn Sill (Peachtree Publishers, Ltd.). Finally head outdoors and see how many birds your little ones spy. Add to the fun by taking along some birdseed or bread crumbs for little ones to leave behind for their feathered friends.

More Ideas For Takin' A Walk

- Invite each child to collect nature items of her choice while walking. Then provide paper plates and glue, and have youngsters make nature collages. On each child's plate, write "I took a walk today!" Send the paper-plate collages home to spark discussion.

- Remind youngsters of the importance of keeping our environment clean. Then take a walk together around your school or center grounds to pick up loose trash, such as cups, plastic bags, and papers. (Caution children to avoid picking up items with sharp edges, such as glass or ripped cans.) Be sure to have everyone scrub their hands when they return to the classroom.

I took a walk today!

Painting

Sock Painting

At last—a use for all those mismatched socks whose mates were "eaten" in the dryer! Collect some extra socks around your house or ask parents for donations. Then gather some kitchen sponges and containers of tempera paint. Roll out a long length of bulletin-board paper on a concrete or blacktop area, and weight down the corners with gallon jugs of water or sand. Place a piece of sponge into each sock toe and tie a knot. Invite each youngster to grasp a sock above the knot, dip the toe into paint until the sponge is soaked, and then paint and print on the paper. Display the finished artwork as a bulletin-board background.

Rock Garden

Gather rocks of all shapes, sizes, and textures. You may want to have little ones take a walk to hunt for rocks, or—if rocks aren't plentiful near your school or center grounds—purchase a bag of landscape rocks at your local home-improvement store. Then set up a table outdoors with containers of tempera paint, brushes, and your rock collection. Encourage youngsters to choose rocks and paint them as they desire. Once the paint dries, designate an area of your playground in which to display your beautiful rock garden.

More Ideas For Painting

- Be sure to protect youngsters' clothing when painting. Use your usual paint smocks, or simply cut head and arm holes in tall kitchen garbage bags and have children slip them on. To protect shoes, have a child slip her feet into small garbage bags, then knot the bags around her ankles. When painting time is over, toss the bags in the trash.
- Outside is the perfect place for tried-and-true favorite art activities like fingerpainting and shaving-cream exploration. Set a Formica®-topped table outdoors and you're ready to let little hands loose!
- Painting doesn't have to involve paint. Set out buckets of water and clean paintbrushes. Invite youngsters to paint a fresh shine on fences, railings, or water fountains. Or have them paint shapes, letters, or numerals on the sidewalk. On a particularly sunny day, this will quickly become a lesson on evaporation!

Tires And Hoops

Tire Path

Ask a local bicycle shop to save you some old bicycle tires. When you've collected several tires, lay them out in a series of ones and twos to create a hop-scotch-like path. Invite youngsters to move along the path by walking, hopping, or jumping. Or use chalk to draw numerals or letters in the circles; then have children toss beanbags into the circles you specify.

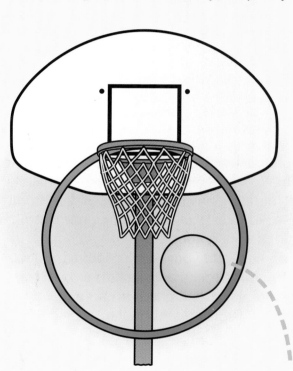

Bigger Than Basketball

If you have some future NBA® All-Stars in your class who can't quite reach the standard hoop yet, try this idea. Hang a hoop over and behind the basket to create a circular opening. Then invite youngsters to toss playground balls through the hoop. Two points!

If you don't have a basketball goal on your play area, ask an adult or older child volunteer to hold a hoop above her head and parallel to the ground to serve as a goal.

More Ideas For Tires And Hoops

- Set up a plastic playground cone as a target, or simply turn a table upside down and use the table legs as targets. Then encourage each of your little ones to toss a bicycle tire or hoop from a specified distance, attempting to get the tire or hoop over the target.
- Have a tire-rolling race. Give each child in a small group a bicycle tire. Set start and finish lines, and have each youngster get rollin'!
- Use hoops as individual play spaces. Invite each child to take a toy or manipulative of her choice and sit inside the outline of a hoop for some solitary playtime.

Boxes And Bags

Who's In The Box?

Gather three sturdy cardboard boxes—each large enough for a child to curl up inside and close the lid. (Computer boxes are usually just right.) To play a game of Who's In The Box?, designate one child to be It. Ask It to close his eyes while three classmates climb into the boxes and close the lids. Then have It open his eyes and ask questions of each child hiding in a box, attempting to figure out their identities. The first child identified becomes It for the next round of play.

Bag Building Blocks

Ask some adult volunteers to help you prepare a set of outdoor building blocks made from paper grocery bags. To make one block, open a grocery bag and stuff it full of crumpled newspaper. Then gently slide another grocery bag over the top of the filled bag. Seal the loose edge with a long strip of packing tape. A set of 10–20 bagblocks will keep youngsters busy building forts and fences, stacking towers, jumping over hurdles, and being generally creative!

More Ideas For Boxes And Bags

- Review positional words by asking a child to get *inside* a box, hop *beside* a box, tiptoe *around* a box, hold a box *over* her head, or hide *behind* a box.
- Open both ends of a few boxes; then tape them together with packing tape to form a tunnel. If desired, cut a few peekaboo holes along the tunnel to let in light. Position the tunnel so that youngsters crawl through it to enter and leave your outdoor play area.
- Open ten paper lunch bags or grocery bags, and stand them bottom-sides-up. Arrange the bags as you would the pins in a game of bowling. Then invite youngsters to take turns rolling a playground ball or tossing a beanbag as they attempt to knock over the bags.

Frozen Fun

Cherry Pops

There's nothing quite like an icy treat on a hot summer day. Gather the ingredients and invite youngsters to help you make a frozen juice snack with a cherry surprise. First prepare a can of frozen lemonade as directed on the can. Add the juice from a jar of maraschino cherries to turn the liquid pink. Divide the liquid into a few small pouring containers that children can handle, such as small, plastic pitchers or creamers. Then give each child a paper cup and a cherry. Have her drop the cherry into the bottom of her cup, then pour in enough juice to cover the cherry, plus a bit more. Add a craft stick to each cup and put the cups in the freezer until firm (about four hours). Twist the frozen snacks out of the cups when you're ready to eat. Don't worry about the crooked handles—just call them Cra-a-zy Crooked Cherry Pops!

Ice-Pop Painting

These inedible ice pops will yield some cool artwork! Half-fill several paper cups with a mixture of half tempera paint and half water. Add a craft stick to each cup and freeze until the mixture is firm (about three hours). When the ice is ready, peel away the cups. Secure a large piece of white bulletin-board paper on a concrete area or on top of a table placed outside. Have youngsters don paint smocks; then hand over the ice-pop paints and let them create! (Be sure to remind them that these ice pops are NOT for eating!) Display the finished artwork with the title "Cool Pop Painting."

More Ideas For Frozen Fun

• Wheel your water table outside. Add ice cubes—plain or colored with food coloring—to the table and let little ones explore.

• On a particularly hot day, experiment with melting times for ice. Set out three clear, plastic cups: one filled with a solid block of ice, one filled with ice cubes, and one filled with crushed ice. Ask youngsters to predict which cup of ice will melt first, second, and last. Check the cups throughout your playtime to see the results.

• Bring in an electric ice-cream freezer and all the ingredients to prepare homemade ice cream. Go through the process as directed by the freezer's manufacturer, encouraging youngsters to help when possible. Then set the freezer in a safe spot near an outdoor electrical outlet and let it churn. When the ice cream is ready later in the day, serve it on cones or in cups—yum!

Movin' Around

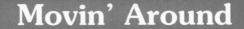

Circle Time

Try this new rendition of the traditional game of Ring Around The Rosie. Have the children form a circle in a large grassy area. Teach them this song and encourage them to move in a clockwise direction around the circle before collapsing in a heap of giggles on the last line of each verse.

(sung to the tune of "Ring Around The Rosie")

> [Walking, walking, walking]
> Out in the summer sun.
> Sunshine, sunshine,
> We all fall down!

Repeat the verse as many times as desired, substituting other action words—such as hopping, jumping, marching, *or* crawling—*for the underlined words.*

Can't Stop Moving!

For this movement activity, ask each child to find his own space, where he is unable to touch anyone else with his arms spread wide. Lead the children in this chant, encouraging them to move in place for the first three lines and then around in a circle on the last line.

> My feet, they won't stop [stomping].
> My feet, they won't stop [stomping].
> My feet, they won't stop [stomping].
> Around in a circle I go.

Repeat the chant as many times as desired, substituting other action words—such as running, hopping, skipping, *or* kicking—*for the underlined word.*

More Ideas For Movin' Around

- Play some tried-and-true games such as Duck Duck Goose, Farmer In The Dell, Hide-And-Seek, or Follow The Leader.
- Invite each child, in turn, to silently choose an animal and perform its movements. Encourage the rest of the group to guess which animal is being imitated.
- Get your little ones movin' around an obstacle course. Set up plastic playground cones or hoops, or draw lines with chalk to delineate a course for youngsters to follow as they walk, hop, jump, or tiptoe. For more of a variation, bring out the tricycles and have little ones drive through the course.

Shapely Sidewalk Chalk

Make your own sidewalk chalk with this simple recipe. Mix two parts plaster of paris with one part liquid tempera paint mixed with water. Pour the resulting mixture into sand molds, candle molds, or a muffin tin to produce chalk with fun, chunky shapes. Or collect empty Squeeze-It® bottles. Cut the bottles in half lengthwise and use the bottle halves as molds. When the chalk has dried, simply pop it out of the molds. Invite little ones to draw on sidewalks or blacktop areas with these fun chalk shapes. Rain or a garden hose will wash the evidence away!

Chalk Paint

For a different artistic experience, mix up a batch of chalk paint for youngsters to use on a sidewalk. In a sand bucket, thoroughly mix together one cup of water, three tablespoons of cornstarch, and a small amount of *washable* paint in the color you desire. Then bring on the brushes and get started! This paint will start out dark and then turn considerably lighter as it dries.

More Ideas For Chalk

- Have youngsters use chalk to draw streets and some surrounding scenery—such as trees, houses, or animals—on a sidewalk or blacktop area. Then bring out some toy cars from your classroom for their driving pleasure!
- Invite each child to lie down on a sidewalk or blacktop while you trace or a friend traces around his body to make a life-sized outline. Then encourage the child to draw and color the outline to resemble his features and clothing.
- Bring out some of your larger stencils from the classroom for youngsters to use with the chalk.

Streamers

Fancy Streamers

These special streamers will have youngsters anxious to test the winds on your playground. To make one streamer, have a child paint the bottom of a thin paper plate with a watercolor design. When the paint is dry, fold the plate in half, unpainted sides together. Cut a three-sided opening about one inch from the fold (through both thicknesses of the paper plate), as shown; then wrap the resulting flaps around the plate's fold and staple them in place. This will create a handle for the streamer. Next staple around the plate's rounded edge; then use a hole puncher to make three to six holes along the rounded edge. Provide several colors of curling ribbon, cut into 18-inch lengths. Invite each child to thread one, two, or three lengths of ribbon through each hole in her plate. Assist each child in tying her ribbons in place.

When these fancy streamers are finished, head outdoors. Encourage little ones to hold their fancy streamers high above their heads and run. What a beautiful sight! When they're not in use, hang these colorful creations from your classroom ceiling.

Wonder Wands

Here's another twist on a simple streamer. Gather six to eight lengths of crepe-paper streamer (or ribbon), each about three feet long. Rubber-band the streamers' ends to one end of a craft stick. If desired, add a few dabs of hot glue for security. Invite each child to hold a finished Wonder Wand by the craft-stick end, then go outside for some movement fun. Encourage youngsters to run with their streamers, circle them overhead, twirl them around their bodies, or use them in a game of Follow the Leader.

More Ideas For Streamers

- Record the streamer shenanigans on video to share with students and their parents.
- Bring a portable tape player and instrumental cassettes outdoors, equip each child with a crepe-paper streamer, and let little ones move to the music.
- Use a long length of crepe-paper streamer or ribbon as a limbo stick, and see just how low your youngsters can go!

23

Homemade Bubbles, Homemade Wands

No need to visit the store when you're ready for some exciting bubble play on a sunny day! Make your own bubble solution by mixing one part Joy® dishwashing liquid with six parts water. Then create your own bubble wands from plastic container lids, such as those for margarine or whipped topping. Simply trim the lip from around each lid so that it lies flat. Then cut holes of various sizes from the lid. Get little ones in on the creation by having them punch holes in the lids with hole punchers. (What a great hand-strengthening exercise!) Clip on clothespins to serve as handles, and your bubble wands are ready to blow!

Bubble Blowers Everywhere!

If the bubble mood strikes you when there's no time to make the bubble wands described in "Homemade Bubbles, Homemade Wands," just invite little ones to look around your classroom for some bubble-blowing equipment. How about the large stringing beads? A plastic bracelet from the housekeeping center? The "0" magnet? A funnel from the sand table? Encourage youngsters to put on their thinking caps as they search your classroom for objects they might be able to blow bubbles through. Then head outdoors with some bubble solution, and see what works and what doesn't. Hey, experimenting is fun!

More Ideas For Bubbles

- Provide spray bottles filled with water. Have children attempt to pop bubbles by squirting them with water.
- Encourage children to blow bubbles *without* a wand. Have a child wet her hands with bubble solution, then make an *o* with one thumb and her index finger. Can she blow a bubble through the opening? Can she form an *o* with both hands and blow a bubble?
- Bubble blowing can be wet and wild! Have each student wear a plastic paint smock, or make a garbage-bag smock for each child following the directions in "More Ideas For Painting" on page 17.

Bringing The Inside Out

Storytime In The Sunshine

Spread an old sheet or blanket on the grass, and gather little ones around to enjoy storytime. Choose a few old favorites, some new books, or some selections with summer as their theme (see the list below). No matter what you read, listening to stories outside in the sunshine will be a fun and different experience for your students.

Summer Legs
Written by Anita Hakkinen
Published by Henry Holt and Company, Inc.

When Summer Comes
Written by Robert Maass
Published by Henry Holt and Company, Inc.

The Summer Noisy Book
Written by Margaret Wise Brown
Published by HarperTrophy

Picnickin'

Another activity that's usually done indoors but is even better done outdoors is eating! For a spontaneous picnic, simply spread a cloth and invite youngsters to enjoy their usual snacks or lunches alfresco. Or plan ahead for a group picnic with donated dishes from parents, paper plates, and a cooler full of juice boxes.

More Ideas For Bringing The Inside Out

- Are there some toys or manipulatives in your classroom that the children have tired of playing with? Bring them outside onto a sheet or a low table, and you'll be amazed at the renewed interest.
- Set up a car wash for your toy vehicles. Partially fill your water table (or a large rubber tub) with soapy water. Set out some water-filled spray bottles and old towels. Then invite youngsters to wash, rinse, and dry!
- How about some outdoor theater? Bring some props outside and have little ones act out a favorite story. Choose a story with an outdoor setting—such as *The Gingerbread Man*—to enjoy the full effect of this daytime drama!

FOOTLOOSE AND FANCY-FREE

Kick off your shoes and jump feetfirst into this unit filled with curriculum-related activities about barefootin'.

by Mackie Rhodes

BAREFOOTIN'

What better way to begin a barefootin' unit than to invite youngsters to bare their soles—the soles of their feet, that is! In advance, send each child home with a copy of the parent letter on page 30. After students bring in the requested items, have each child remove his shoes and socks. Instruct him to wet his washcloth, then wring the excess water from it. Squirt a small amount of liquid soap onto his cloth. Have the child wash, then towel-dry, his feet thoroughly. As youngsters wash their feet, encourage them to say this "sole-ful" chant, whispering the word *barefootin'* each time it is recited.

Take your soap and water, and
scrub your feet clean.
Barefootin'. *(pause)* Barefootin'.
A-rub 'em and a-scrub 'em. You're
a foot-cleaning machine!
Barefootin'. *(pause)* Barefootin'.
Grab a towel. Dry 'em quick. The
cleanest feet you've ever seen.
Barefootin'. *(pause)* Barefootin'.
Two fancy-free feet with a sparkle
and a sheen!
Barefootin'. *(pause)* Barefootin'.

FANCY FOOTWORK

Challenge youngsters to put their best feet forward in this no-hands activity. To begin, divide your class into student pairs. Tell youngsters that you have some really hard jobs for them to do; then assign each pair a simple task to complete, such as assembling a puzzle, building a block tower, looking at a book, or drawing a picture. When the partners comment on how easy their assignments seem, "suddenly remember" to tell them that they cannot use their hands to do the tasks. They must use only their feet! After each student pair succeeds at its task (or decides that it cannot be accomplished using only feet), assign a different task to the partners, rotating the assignments so that each pair has an opportunity to try several different tasks. Afterward discuss the ease or difficulty with which students performed the tasks with their feet. Look, Ma! No hands!

REFLECTIONS OF THE SOLE

Encourage youngsters' story recall skills with this idea that truly mirrors their soles. Ask each student or student pair to select a rhyme or story, such as "Two Little Blackbirds" or *The Three Little Pigs.* Using washable markers, help each child decorate the sole of each of her feet to represent a different character from the rhyme or story. Then have the student(s) sit in front of a floor mirror so that she (they) can see the reflected soles of her (their) feet—or foot puppets. Encourage the child(ren) to practice performing the rhyme/story with the foot puppet reflections in the mirror. If desired, invite students to perform their rhymes/stories with their puppets facing the class.

PIGGY PAINTING

What else can little piggies do other than going to the market or eating roast beef? Why, paint a passel of pretty colors, of course! To introduce youngsters to the primary colors and color combinations, read *Mouse Paint* by Ellen Stoll Walsh (Harcourt Brace & Company). Remind students that the mice in the story mixed the paint colors with their feet; then invite students to use their feet to do a little piggy painting of their own. To prepare, spread out a length of bulletin-board paper on the floor. Put a small amount of each color of fingerpaint—red, blue, and yellow—on the paper; then have a child step barefoot into two different paint colors. Encourage him to mix the colors with his feet to create a new color. What color did his little piggies make? After the child finishes mixing colors, ask him to remove the excess paint from his feet with a disposable wipe, then wash and dry his feet thoroughly. Or, if desired, extend this activity with "Dogs Come In All Sizes."

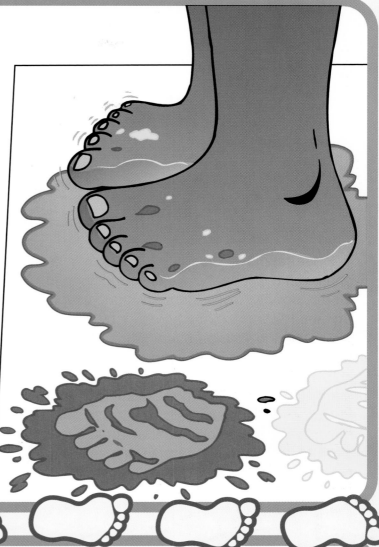

DOGS COME IN ALL SIZES

If youngsters participated in "Piggy Painting," you might have them extend that activity with this foot-printing idea. Before each child washes the paint from his feet, ask him to make a footprint on a sheet of construction paper. After his footprint dries, have him carefully cut around the outline of the print, then label the back of his cutout with his name. Collect all the cutouts in a large shoe; then place the shoe in a math center. To use the center, tell students that a commonly used word for feet is *dogs*. Then, as student pairs visit this center, encourage them to sequence the footprints—or dogs—by size. It's true: dogs come in all different sizes!

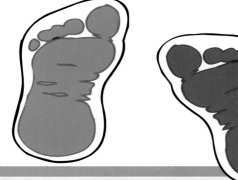

27

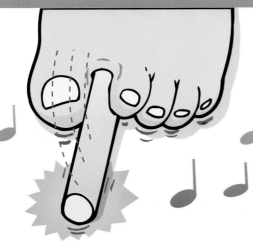

Toe Jammin'

A toe-tappin' good time awaits your little ones with this idea. To warm youngsters up for this activity, invite them to imitate simple rhythmic patterns that you create by stomping or tapping your bare feet. Then increase the difficulty by foot-clapping rhythms for students to repeat. Afterward challenge students to imitate the patterns using rhythm instruments—such as bells, rhythm sticks, or cymbals—held between their toes. Conclude your toe-jammin' session with an invitation for youngsters to make the barefootin' music of their choice to accompany some lively recordings.

Do The Walk!

Can you do the walk? Challenge youngsters to perform creative walk patterns with this activity. To begin, show students the *heel, ball, sides,* and *toes* of your bare feet; then have the children point to these parts on their own feet. After youngsters are familiar with the foot vocabulary, ask them to watch you walk on just your heels or your toes, or one of the other named parts. Then invite youngsters to imitate your walk. After they practice walking on the different parts of their feet, have students gather into small groups. Ask a leader to guide her group through an obstacle course as they walk on an assigned foot part. Let's do the walk!

Texture Talk

Build youngsters' descriptive vocabulary when you introduce them, feetfirst, to a variety of textures. In advance, duplicate and cut from tagboard one copy of the foot pattern on page 30 for each texture to be represented, such as sand, rice, play dough, fingerpaint, plastic grass, or wood chips. Create a sample of each texture on a separate foot cutout; then attach two wiggle eyes and a pipe-cleaner mouth near the toe end of each cutout. Mount each textured cutout onto a separate large sheet of construction paper labeled with the texture's name. Then partially fill a separate large box lid (or tray) with each of the different textured substances. Invite each student, in turn, to step barefoot into each box lid. Ask him to describe the feeling of the substance's texture. Record his responses in speech bubbles on the sheet representing the corresponding textured cutout. Afterward display the finished miniposters on a bulletin board with the title "Texture Talk: 'Feeturing' [teacher's name]'s Class." If desired, add to this display with photos you snapped during your little ones' texture exploration.

FROLICKING FEET

Enhance youngsters' observation skills while creating in them a new appreciation for the many movements of their feet. To begin, have youngsters sit on the floor and lift their feet into the air. Ask them to examine the different ways their feet move. Then help youngsters identify the parts of their feet—the *toes, balls, arches, heels, sides, soles,* and *ankles.* Ask a volunteer to stand up and move around the room in a suggested fashion, such as walking, jumping, or skating. Have the rest of the class watch his feet closely as he moves. What individual foot actions make it possible for that child to move in that way? After each discussion, invite the entire class to perform the same action, in follow-the-leader fashion, paying particular attention to the different foot movements involved. Wow! These fine-tuned actions make for fun, frolicking feet.

HOT POTATO, TOOTSY-STYLE

Here's a ticklish circle game designed to promote group cooperation, quick problem solving, and lots of laughter. Have youngsters sit in a circle of chairs facing one another. Explain that they will play a game of Hot Potato, but instead of passing the potato with their hands, they will pass it with their feet. Create a small potato from a crumpled piece of paper; then have students pass the potato feet-to-feet around the circle. Chorally count the number of passes made before the potato is dropped. If desired, invite each child who successfully completes the pass to give himself a round of foot-applause. Ready, set, pass! And no tootsy-tickling allowed!

Empress skin lotion

Baby Powder

PAMPERED "PEDS"

Expand the vocabulary of your little ones just a little further as they indulge in a bit of foot-pampering. Just prior to rest time, tell your class that when *ped* is heard in a word, it is usually in reference to the foot or feet. For example, a *pedestrian* is someone who travels by foot. Or a bike or car *pedal* is operated by a foot. Then, if desired, have youngsters wash their feet again, as in "Barefootin' " on page 26. Invite students to gently rub lotion and/or powder on all the different parts of their feet, informing them that when they take care of their feet in this way, they are giving themselves a type of *pedicure.* Ahhh! Feels good. Now put those "peds" to bed.

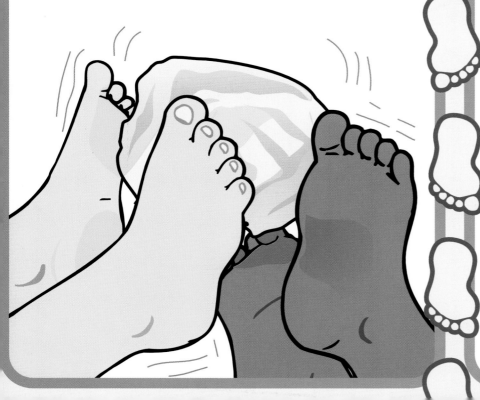

Parent Letter
Use with "Barefootin' " on page 26.

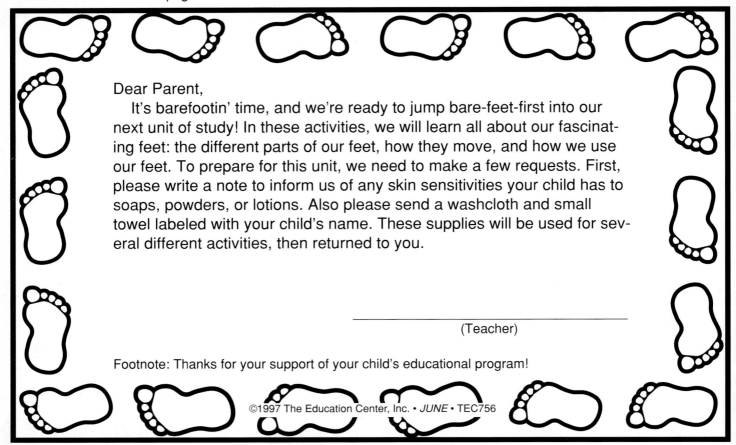

Dear Parent,

It's barefootin' time, and we're ready to jump bare-feet-first into our next unit of study! In these activities, we will learn all about our fascinating feet: the different parts of our feet, how they move, and how we use our feet. To prepare for this unit, we need to make a few requests. First, please write a note to inform us of any skin sensitivities your child has to soaps, powders, or lotions. Also please send a washcloth and small towel labeled with your child's name. These supplies will be used for several different activities, then returned to you.

_____
(Teacher)

Footnote: Thanks for your support of your child's educational program!

Foot Pattern
Use with "Texture Talk" on page 28.

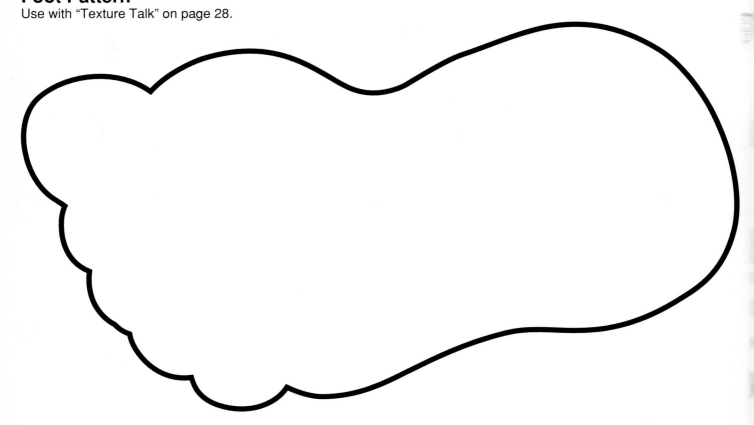

Look—Ladybugs!

Youngsters will go buggy over this unit on those pretty polka-dotted inhabitants of the garden—ladybugs! So ask them to flit on over and explore these ever-so-interesting insects.

ideas contributed by Diane Gilliam

A Ladybug Hunt

Prepare an indoor ladybug hunt to introduce your students to some facts about ladybugs. First duplicate ten copies of the ladybug pattern on page 35 onto red construction paper. Cut out the patterns; then staple an equal-sized, white paper circle behind each cutout. Then fold each ladybug cutout up, as shown, and write a ladybug fact from "Buggy—But True" on the white circle below it. Hide the completed ladybugs around your classroom—or around your school or center—where little ones can spot them.

When you are ready to begin your ladybug unit, inform youngsters that they will be going on a ladybug hunt. Show them a large, clear jar and explain that you'll be collecting the ladybugs they find in this jar for further study. Then lead the way, perhaps spotting the first paper ladybug yourself to get things started. After your students have collected all the ladybugs you've hidden, return to your circle area and ask volunteers to pull the ladybugs from the jar, one at a time, as you share the fact printed on each one. If desired, share drawings or photos from a good nonfiction book to further your discussion. Have youngsters tell about their own experiences with and observations of ladybugs. Then, if desired, engage little ones in painting a flower-garden mural. Post the mural on a bulletin board, and add the ladybug cutouts and a title that reads "Ladybug Lingo."

Ladybugs are colorful beetles.

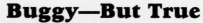

Buggy—But True

- Ladybugs are colorful beetles.
- Ladybugs have three body parts, two antennae, and six legs.
- A ladybug's transparent wings are hidden beneath hard wing cases.
- Ladybugs can be red, orange, yellow, or black.
- Ladybugs can have anywhere from 0 to 22 spots.
- A ladybug's favorite food is aphids.
- A ladybug can eat 100 aphids a day.
- Some ladybugs protect themselves from birds by playing dead.
- One ladybug can lay hundreds of eggs.
- Many ladybugs hibernate during the winter.

Paper-Plate Puppets

Reinforce the appearance of a ladybug and strengthen fine-motor skills with this paper-plate project. Provide each youngster with a thin white paper plate, crayons, some black construction-paper scraps, scissors, glue, eight black pipe-cleaner halves, and a 1" x 6" strip of black construction paper. Show the children how to draw black lines on each plate to resemble a ladybug's head and two wing cases. (You may want to do this in advance for younger children.) Instruct each child to color her plate as shown. Then invite her to cut any number of small circles from the black paper before gluing them in place on the wing cases. Assist each child in punching three holes on each side of her ladybug and two on the head. Then have her thread a pipe-cleaner half through each hole and twist its ends together to create six legs and two antennae. Finally staple each child's 1" x 6" strip to the back of her plate to create a handle for her ladybug puppet.

Encourage little ones to manipulate their puppets as they sing "I'm A Ladybug" (to the tune of "Found A Peanut"). Are your little beetles ready for Broadway?

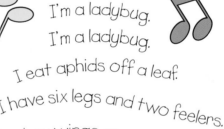

I'm a ladybug.
I'm a ladybug.
I eat aphids off a leaf.
I have six legs and two feelers.
And my wings are underneath.

Bake Up A Batch Of Bugs

Your little ladybug lovers will be scurrying to taste these scrumptious cupcakes! Either in advance or with your students' help, prepare a batch of strawberry cupcakes from your favorite cake mix. Then have each child frost a cupcake with vanilla frosting. Have him carefully roll the top of his cupcake in a container of red sugar crystals. Then provide each youngster with a six-inch length of licorice lace and a few chocolate chips. Demonstrate how to use pieces of licorice to form the ladybug's head and wing cases. The chocolate chips will serve as spots. If desired, provide Runt® candies, and have each child use these to form eyes and a mouth on his ladybug. Then invite youngsters to enjoy their cupcake creations while you read aloud *The Grouchy Ladybug* by Eric Carle (HarperCollins Children's Books).

Life Cycle Of A Ladybug

Have your youngsters studied the metamorphosis of a butterfly? Then they'll be fascinated to learn that ladybugs, too, have a larval life cycle. In advance, prepare the materials to help each student create a growth wheel that illustrates this life cycle. For each child, stack two six-inch paper plates together. Use sharp scissors to poke a hole through the centers of the two plates; then attach them with a brad. Cut a pie-shaped wedge from the top plate as shown, being careful to avoid the center. Print the words "The Ladybug Life Cycle" on each of the top plates. Then, if desired, duplicate the illustrations on page 35 for each child.

Share *The Ladybug And Other Insects* (A First Discovery Book) by Gallimard Jeunesse and Pascale de Bourgoing (Scholastic Inc.) for a clear and concise description of the ladybug's life cycle. On a sheet of chart paper, sketch the five stages in a circular flowchart (or use enlarged copies of the reproducible illustrations on page 35). Model how to retell the life cycle of the ladybug, using the pictures as cues. Invite some student volunteers to retell the life cycle using your chart.

Then have each youngster make his own growth wheel. Distribute the prepared plates. In the open space below the cutout wedge, have each child either draw or glue the duplicated illustration for the first stage. Then have him rotate the top plate until that picture can no longer be seen. He is then ready to draw or glue his second illustration. Have students continue until they've illustrated (or colored, cut, and glued) all five stages and numbered them accordingly. Then assess their understanding by having them use the growth wheels to describe the ladybug's life cycle.

Stage 1: A ladybug lays *eggs* on the bottom of a leaf.

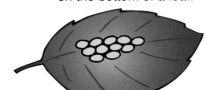

Stage 2: Larvae hatch out of the eggs and begin to eat aphids.

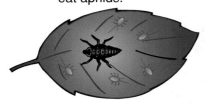

Stage 3: Each larva grows bigger and sheds its skin.

Stage 4: A larva attaches itself under a leaf and sheds its skin once more. It is now called a pupa.

Stage 5: A few days later, a ladybug emerges from the pupa.

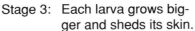

Ladybugs To The Rescue!

You've told little ones that ladybugs like to eat aphids. Now explain why that ladybug diet is so beneficial to humans. Read *What About Ladybugs?* by Celia Godkin (Sierra Club Books For Children) or simply explain that aphids are pesky little bugs that enjoy sucking the juices out of plants and flowers. Aphids can destroy a vegetable or flower garden if left to their own devices, and gardeners often bring in ladybugs to control the aphid population.

Invite youngsters to create a garden scene with some beany buggy art to remind them of the ladybug's importance. In advance, spread a bag of dried lima beans on sheets of newspaper and spray-paint one side of the beans red. When the paint is dry, provide each child in a small group with some painted beans, a sheet of light blue construction paper, an assortment of construction-paper scraps, scissors, glue, and a black permanent marker. Invite the children to make garden scenes by cutting and tearing construction-paper shapes, and gluing them onto the light blue backgrounds. Then show children how to use the black marker to decorate a red-painted bean so that it resembles a ladybug. Have them glue a few ladybugs to their garden scenes. Have each child finish her project by writing or dictating a sentence about ladybugs in the open space at the top of her paper.

Ladybugs are good because they eat aphids. NATHANiel

La-La-La-Ladybug

Teach youngsters this song and its accompanying motions. Then encourage them to sing the song for their families and share all they've learned about ladybugs.

I'm A Bug
(sung to the tune of "I'm A Nut")

I eat aphids; don't you know?	*Point to chest with thumbs.*
I eat aphids so I'll grow.	*Make muscles with both arms.*
I eat aphids; they're the best!	*Rub tummy.*
They're for me; don't want the rest.	*Shake head "no" and hold palm out to indicate "stop."*
I'm a bug.	*Clap, clap.*
I'm a bug.	*Clap, clap.*
Ladybug, ladybug, ladybug.	*Clap, clap.*

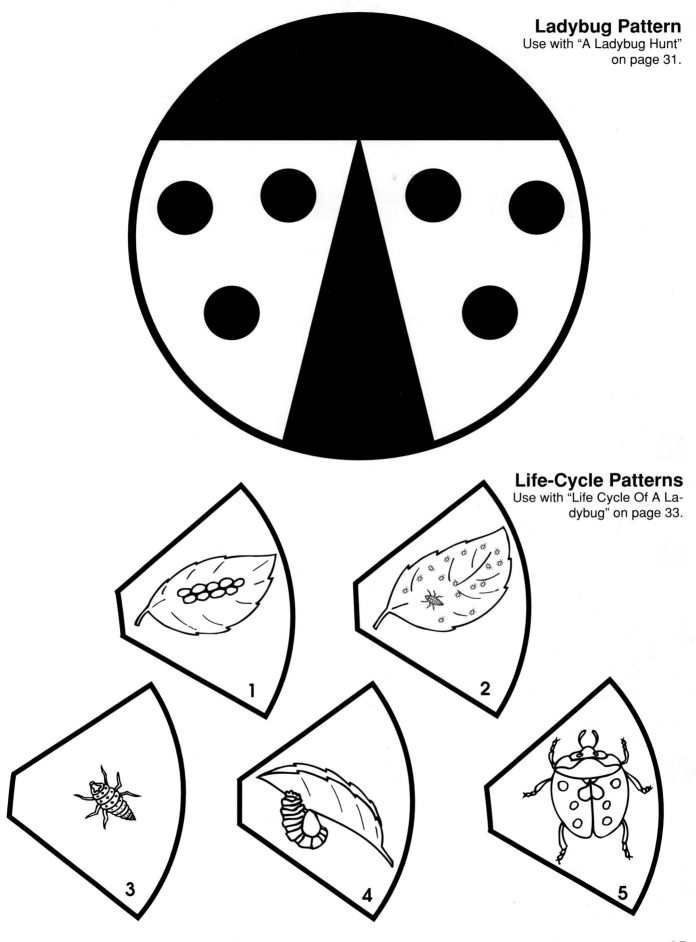

Ladybug Pattern
Use with "A Ladybug Hunt" on page 31.

Life-Cycle Patterns
Use with "Life Cycle Of A Ladybug" on page 33.

1

2

3

4

5

HAVE YOU "HERD"? IT'S DAIRY MONTH!

Dairy Month comes only once a year, in the very dairy month of June. Celebrate with this "cowabunga" collection of activities your little ones are sure to enjoy!

ideas contributed by Vicki Mockaitis Pacchetti

WHO MAKES MILK?

Do your youngsters know where milk and dairy products come from? Find out what they know; then add to their knowledge when you share *The Milk Makers* by Gail Gibbons (Simon & Schuster Children's Books). This factual book details how cows go about the business of making milk and how people go about the business of processing it. Preschoolers will especially enjoy this book as a Reading Rainbow® video, complete with a video field trip to a California dairy farm and a lesson in milking by hand. Check your local or school library to see if it's available or order it from GPN by calling 1-800-228-4630.

OUR VERY OWN COW

Now that little ones know that cows are the source of that yummy milk and all those delightful dairy products, they may want to get to know cows a bit better. Contact Stonyfield Farm Yogurt about the company's "Have A Cow!" program. Call 1-800-PRO-COWS (M–F 9 A.M.–5 P.M. ET) to sponsor a cow for your class! For a small fee, you'll receive a sponsorship certificate, a photo of your class's cow, a biography about the cow's life on the farm, and updates through an annual "moosletter." Won't your students be excited to have their very own cow?

MAPPING THE MILK MAKERS

Encourage older students to "moo-ve" into beginning geography skills by marking the major milk-producing states on a map. In advance use a cow stamp, cow stickers, or copies of the cow mini-pattern on page 44 to embellish five sticky notes. Then gather your students around a large map of the United States. Begin by helping them find your home state. Inform students that every state has some dairy farms, but there are a few states that are overflowing with milk makers. Ask youngsters to locate Wisconsin, California, New York, Minnesota, and Pennsylvania on the map. Help volunteers affix a cow-covered sticky note to each of these states. Ask youngsters to locate which of these states is closest to your home state. Point out that not only is milk nutritious and delicious, but it also provides many people—particularly those in the marked states—with their livelihood.

MINI-MILKERS

Perhaps you live in a dairy state or know of a dairy farm nearby. Plan a field trip to give youngsters a firsthand look at cows and milk production. If you can't visit a dairy farm where little ones can get a grip on milking by hand, try this "udder-ly" fascinating simulation.

Collect a few latex medical gloves. Gently puff a bit of air into each glove; then take a straight pin and poke two of the fingertips. Mark these two fingertips with a permanent marker to distinguish them from the others. Then fill the glove with a thin solution of white tempera paint and water. Use a rubber band to secure the wrist opening of the glove tightly. Prepare three or four gloves in this manner, and divide your class into groups for this activity. Then hold a glove over a bucket or over your classroom sink and demonstrate for a small group of youngsters how to grasp one of the marked fingers near the top and gently pull downward to make the liquid squirt out. Give every child a turn to try his hand at this makeshift milking.

A "MOO-TRITIOUS" MILK BOOKLET

Inform students that milk contains the six nutrients humans need for growth and good health: water, carbohydrates, fats, proteins, vitamins, and minerals. These nutrients help us grow, give us energy, prevent disease, and strengthen bones and teeth.

Have each child make a booklet to review the benefits of drinking milk. To prepare the booklets, first make one copy of the cow pattern on page 42. Write the title "Milk Is 'Moo-tritious!' " and the words "Illustrated by _____ " within the outline of the cow. Then program each of three blank sheets of copy paper with one of the following sentences:

Page 1: Milk is good for our bones.
Page 2: Milk gives us energy.
Page 3: Milk helps us grow.

Then duplicate a class supply of the programmed cover and pages on white construction paper. Prepare the materials and set out the supplies necessary for each child to complete her booklet pages as described below:

Cover: Write your name on the blank line. Color the cow.
Page 1: Use a white crayon to draw a stick figure of a person. Paint over your drawing with black watercolor to reveal the "bones."
Page 2: Cut out a magazine picture of someone engaged in a physical activity. Glue it on the page.
Page 3: Draw a picture of yourself. Next to your drawing, glue a strip of yellow construction paper marked with black lines to resemble a measuring tape.

When all the pages are complete and the paint and glue have dried, sequence and staple each child's booklet pages together with the cover on top. Invite youngsters to take their booklets home and share their nutrition knowledge with their families.

MILK EVERY DAY

Nutrition experts recommend that children drink at least three 8-ounce glasses of milk a day. To encourage each of your little ones to drink up, send home a copy of the motivational chart on page 43. Ask that each child return the completed chart the next week. Present all those who fill out the chart a copy of the award badge from page 43 to color and wear. If any of your students have milk allergies, encourage them to discuss what foods they substitute to get the nutrients of milk. Ask their parents to help them fill out their charts, noting the substitutions.

SHAKE, RATTLE, AND BUTTER SOME ROLLS!

Milk isn't the only wonderful food that comes from dairy cows. Introduce your little ones to another dairy favorite—butter—with this activity. To prepare, bring in a clean jar with a screw-on lid, a pint of heavy cream, and some small rolls.

Gather your little ones into a circle and explain that many of the foods we eat are made from milk. Tell them that butter is made from cream, the fatty part of milk that is sometimes skimmed—or separated—from fresh milk before it is processed. Show students the cream and the jar and invite them to help you make some butter. Pour the cream into the jar and seal the lid tightly. Demonstrate how to hold the jar with both hands and shake it vigorously. Then pass the jar around the circle, encouraging each child to shake it while the class repeats this chant:

Shake it, shake it, shake it, high and low;
Shaking cream makes butter, you know!

After every child has shaken the jar, check the consistency of the cream. If necessary, send the jar for another shaky trip around the circle until it separates into pale yellow clumps. Then pour off the remaining liquid. Spread a bit of homemade butter on a roll for each child.

DAIRY DELIGHTFUL SNACK

Chances are, dairy foods are among your students' favorites. So plan a tasting party on a special "Dairy Delight Day." Several days in advance, duplicate the parent note on page 44 for each child to take home. Fill in the date and the blanks on the note to request specific dairy items from each child's family. On the designated day, set out the dairy foods and encourage youngsters to try a little taste of each one. Then follow up this delicious dairy feast with the activity described in "Dairy Druthers."

DAIRY DRUTHERS

After your tasting party (described in "Dairy Delightful Snack"), create a class graph to reveal your youngsters' favorite dairy foods. Prepare an open graph on your chalkboard or a large piece of bulletin-board paper. Label the graph "Our Favorite Dairy Foods" and label each column with the name of a dairy food your students tasted. To make graph markers, duplicate and cut out a class supply of the cow and milk mini-patterns on page 44. Give each child a mini-pattern to color and label with her name. Then assist each child in adding her marker to the graph under the heading of her choice. (Use Sticky-Tac or rolled tape to affix the graph markers.) Discuss the results of your graph. To extend this activity on another day, have each student graph her favorite type of cheese, favorite ice-cream flavor, or favorite type of milk.

DAIRY-O

Use this fun version of lotto to remind students of the wealth of dairy foods. Duplicate several copies of the gameboard on page 45. To make different versions of the gameboard, cut all but one board so that each has only nine squares, as shown. Next cut the remaining board into individual squares to serve as the calling cards. If desired, mount the gameboards and calling cards on tagboard and laminate them for durability.

To play a game of Dairy-O, give each child in a small group a gameboard and nine milk-jug lids to use as markers. Stack the calling cards in front of you. Draw a calling card and either call out the name of the dairy food pictured, or simply display the card for the group to see. Any player who has that food pictured on his gameboard may place a milk-jug lid over that square. The first player to cover all the squares on his card calls out, "Dairy-O!"

VERY DAIRY VOCABULARY

Build students' vocabulary skills and provide practice with beginning sounds when you make this matching game. Begin by asking youngsters to generate a list of dairy-related words, such as *cow, milk, cheese,* and *ice cream.* Write each word at one end of a sentence strip. At the opposite end of each strip, use a sticker, a rubber stamp, or a magazine picture to illustrate the word. Then make a puzzle cut between the word and the illustration. Place all the strips in a center; then ask youngsters to match the words and pictures, using beginning letters as clues.

MILK-MAC-MOO

Get little ones contemplating their next "moo-ves" with this dairy variation of Tic-Tac-Toe. In advance, prepare a few Tic-Tac-Toe-type grids on colored construction paper or tagboard. For each gameboard, duplicate five of the cow mini-patterns and five of the milk mini-patterns on page 44 to create a complete set of ten cards. Laminate all the boards and cards for durability, if desired. Store each game set in a zippered plastic bag. Invite a pair of students to share a game set and follow the rules of Tic-Tac-Toe, substituting cows and milk cartons for *X*s and *O*s.

DAIRY FACTS ON DISPLAY

The bulletin-board breed of cattle on this display will help little ones recall important facts they've learned about dairy foods. To create the display, first cover a bulletin board with light blue background paper. Add a strip of green paper along the bottom of the board to represent grass. Fringe the green paper, if desired, to add a three-dimensional effect. Then duplicate a class supply of the cow pattern on page 42 on white construction paper. Provide black ink pads or shallow trays of black tempera paint. Direct each youngster to cut out his cow, then make black thumbprints all over his cutout. After the ink or paint has dried, staple the finished Holsteins to the bulletin board. If you wish, add more dimension to the display with a craft-stick fence and a barn made by covering a half-gallon milk carton with red construction paper and adding black marker details.

Next cut a class supply of speech bubbles from half-sheets of white paper. Ask each child to dictate one fact he has learned during your Dairy Month unit as you write his response on a speech-bubble cutout. Staple each child's speech bubble above his cow. Finally, add the title "Have You 'Herd'? " What a "moo-velous" way to review what your little ones have learned!

DAIRY BOOKS YOUR CLASS WILL "UDDER-LY" LOVE

No Moon, No Milk!
Written by Chris Babcock
Published by Crown Books For Young Readers

Extra Cheese, Please!
   Mozzarella's Journey From Cow To Pizza
Written by Cris Peterson
Published by Boyds Mills Press, Inc.

Brown Cow, Green Grass, Yellow Mellow Sun
Written by Ellen Jackson
Published by Hyperion Books For Children

Counting Cows
Written by Woody Jackson
Published by Harcourt
   Brace & Company

Belinda
Written by Pamela Allen
Published by Puffin Books

Cow Pattern

Use with "A 'Moo-tritious' Milk Booklet" on page 38 and "Dairy Facts On Display" on page 41.

1, 2, 3...MILK FOR ME!

Draw a happy face 😊 in each space when you drink a glass of milk.

	Monday	Tuesday	Wednesday	Thursday	Friday	Saturday	Sunday
1							
2							
3							

Cow And Milk Mini-Patterns

Use with "Mapping The Milk Makers" on page 37, "Dairy Druthers" on page 39, and "Milk-Mac-Moo" on page 40.

Parent Note

Use with "Dairy Delightful Snack" on page 39.

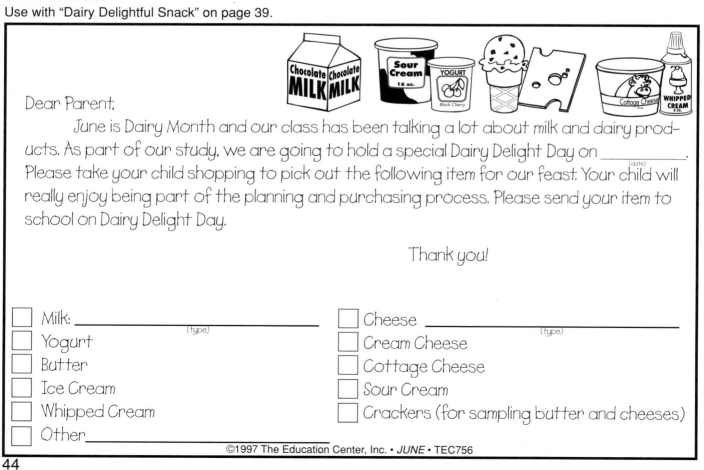

Dear Parent,

    June is Dairy Month and our class has been talking a lot about milk and dairy products. As part of our study, we are going to hold a special Dairy Delight Day on _____.
    (date)
Please take your child shopping to pick out the following item for our feast. Your child will really enjoy being part of the planning and purchasing process. Please send your item to school on Dairy Delight Day.

                              Thank you!

- [ ] Milk: _____ (type)
- [ ] Yogurt
- [ ] Butter
- [ ] Ice Cream
- [ ] Whipped Cream
- [ ] Other_____

- [ ] Cheese _____ (type)
- [ ] Cream Cheese
- [ ] Cottage Cheese
- [ ] Sour Cream
- [ ] Crackers (for sampling butter and cheeses)

'Tis The Season...For Sharks!

Usually just the word *shark* sends shivers down the spines of young and old. While these fierce fish are to be respected, they shouldn't be feared. Armed with the knowledge learned in this unit, little ones will see that sharks can be friendly, ferocious, *and* fun! So grab your gear and dive in! The water's fine—or is it?

ideas contributed by Lucia Kemp Henry

Shark Smarts

How much do your students already know about sharks? Find out with this activity. Using the patterns on page 52 as a reference, cut out a large shark shape from gray construction paper. Show your youngsters a poster, photo, or toy replica of a shark. On the shark cutout, list all the children's comments that the picture or toy evokes. Sort through the fact and fiction by reading a simple shark fact book, such as *Hungry, Hungry Sharks* by Joanna Cole (Random House Books For Young Readers). Then go back over the list with your youngsters. Cross out any false information and add any new information that students learn. Keep the cutout handy throughout the unit to revisit and modify.

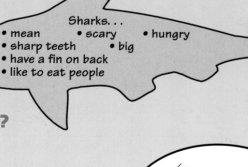

Sharks...
• mean   • scary   • hungry
• sharp teeth   • big
• have a fin on back
• like to eat people

Poetry In Motion

Teach your students this poem to reinforce their new knowledge of the shark family. Add the optional motions to have little ones swimmin' in time to the rhyme.

What Is A Shark?

What is a shark?
A shark is a creature,
That many big zoos
And aquariums feature!

What is a shark?
A shark is a beastie,
That dines every day
At a little fish feastie.

What is a shark?
A shark's a big fishy,
That swims in the sea,
With a splash and a splishy.

What is a shark?
A shark's *not* a meanie,
And it comes in all sizes—
From giant to teeny!

Those Amazing Fish

Share these interesting shark facts with your little ones. First ask each question and encourage children to respond with a thumbs-up for yes or a thumbs-down for no. Then read the fact that follows. Wow, I didn't know that!

- Are sharks fish?

  Yes, sharks account for at least 340 kinds of fish.
- Do sharks have bones?

  No, shark skeletons are made of cartilage, the material found at the tip of your nose and around your ears.
- Do sharks eat only fish?

  No, sharks eat seals, turtles, fish, birds, crabs, whales, plants, and even garbage!
- Is a shark the biggest fish in the sea?

  Yes, the whale shark is the largest shark and also the largest fish in the sea.
- Do sharks eat each other?

  Yes, most sharks are aggressive eaters that will attack members of their own kind.
- Do sharks have scales?

  Yes, sharks have small, sharp, pointed scales.
- Can you see a shark's fin when the shark is swimming near the top of the water?

  No, the dorsal fin rarely shows when the shark is near the water's surface.
- Do people eat sharks?

  Yes, people have eaten sharks for a long time. They also make a soup from shark fins.

A Sea Of Skills

Take a bite out of practicing math skills by using sharks as manipulatives. Reproduce a supply of the large and small shark patterns on page 52 onto construction paper. Cut out the shark shapes; then use them for the following activities:

- Draw two large circles on a piece of poster board and label them as shown. Glue a large shark cutout in one circle and a small shark cutout in the other circle. Give a student an assortment of the cutouts and instruct her to sort the sharks by size.

- Have students create simple patterns with the big and little sharks; then glue the patterns onto blue construction-paper strips. (For more advanced students, vary the color of the shark shapes.) If desired, use the shark strips as a "fin-tastic" border for the shark mural described in "Be Wary Of These Waters" on page 49.

- Reinforce measuring skills by encouraging youngsters to use the small shark cutouts as nonstandard units of measure. Have each child, or pair of children, measure an object in the classroom by positioning the cutouts end to end.

- Make up some shark stories to spark some critical thinking; then have small groups of students use the shark cutouts to "lurk" for a solution. For example, "Two large sharks feasted on five smaller sharks. One of the sharks ate two. How many did the other shark eat?"

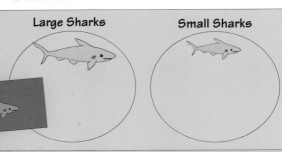

Large Sharks   Small Sharks

Opposite Attack!

Learning opposites is a breeze when little ones use sharks to attack this sometimes difficult concept. Duplicate the big and little shark patterns from page 52 onto construction paper for each child. Have the child color and cut out the shark shapes; then have him tape each one to the end of a different craft stick to make a simple puppet. Encourage him to manipulate his puppets according to the directions in the following chant:

> Big shark, little shark, swim up high. Big shark, little shark, swim down low.
> Big shark, little shark, swim so fast. Big shark, little shark, swim so slow.
> Big shark, little shark, swim in front. Big shark, little shark, swim behind.
> Big shark, little shark, swim zigzags. Big shark, little shark, swim a straight line.

Showy Sharks

Invite each youngster to make one of these flashy sharks to help him remember some of the shark's unique characteristics. To prepare for this activity, each child will need a 4" x 12" sandpaper rectangle, a one-inch wiggle eye, a seven-inch length of small white rickrack, a six-inch length of black yarn, and access to paints and sponges. Explain to students that sharks, unlike most other fish, are covered in scales that are sharp and rough, have open gills instead of covered gills to help them breathe, and have several rows of teeth. Show shark photos from a reference book. Have a volunteer count the gills of several sharks (most have five gills). While viewing the shark photos, also point out the different colors and patterns of sharks.

To make a shark, direct each child to cut a triangle from one of the short ends of his sandpaper rectangle. Then have him glue the triangle to one of the long sides to make a fin. Encourage the child to sponge-paint his shark to resemble the color or pattern of a real shark. While the paint is drying, instruct him to cut the rickrack (teeth) to fit his shark's mouth and to cut the yarn into five pieces to make gills. After the paint dries, assist him in gluing the eye, teeth, and gills onto his shark. Display these showy sharks on the background created in "Be Wary Of These Waters" on page 49.

Here Fishy, Fishy!

Give your hungry sharks a chance to catch tasty fish in this fun game. Have three volunteers be the Sharks and the rest of the class start out as Fish. Instruct the Sharks to form a small circle, hold fins (hands), and lift up their arms. Then tell the Sharks to begin rotating their circle. To play the game, play some lively music and have the Fish "swim" in and out of the circle, under the Sharks' fins. When the music stops, instruct the Sharks to stop moving and lower their fins. Any Fish caught in the middle of the circle become Sharks and join the circle. Continue playing until all of the Fish are gobbled up. Chomp, chomp!

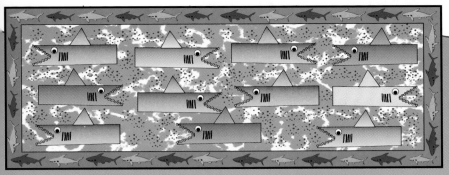

Be Wary Of These Waters

Your youngsters will get plenty of fine-motor practice while creating these treacherous waters. Lay a bulletin-board-sized length of white paper on a newspaper-covered floor. Divide your class into three groups. Set out a few pans of watered-down, dark blue paint; then have one group of students use small rollers to paint the paper in horizontal strokes. After this paint dries, have another group of children sponge-paint on top of the rolled paint with light blue paint. Allow this paint to dry; then have the last third of your class use white paint and brushes to spatter-paint a final layer. When the paint dries, hang the background on a bulletin board. Infest the water with youngsters' sharks made in "Showy Sharks" on page 48. If desired, border this shark mural with the pattern strips created in "A Sea Of Skills" on page 47. Absolutely *no swimming* allowed here!

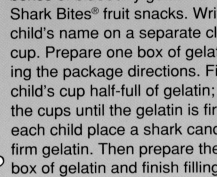

Sharks For Snack?

You bet! Nothing could be tastier than a mouthful of seawater with a hint of shark. Help your little shark lovers make these swimmy treats from two boxes of blueberry gelatin and a box of Shark Bites® fruit snacks. Write each child's name on a separate clear plastic cup. Prepare one box of gelatin following the package directions. Fill each child's cup half-full of gelatin; then chill the cups until the gelatin is firm. Have each child place a shark candy on the firm gelatin. Then prepare the second box of gelatin and finish filling up each youngster's cup. Chill again until firm. Then watch your youngsters mimic a shark's feeding frenzy!

Dinnertime!

Teach your little ones this fingerplay for some deep-sea counting fun. Be glad you're not a fish!

Shark sees some fish	*Point to your eyes.*
Swimming in the sea.	*Make swimming motion with your hand.*
Shark eats one fish,	*Hold up one finger.*
Happy as can be!	*Point to your smiling face.*
Shark eats two fish.	*Hold up two fingers.*
Any more in sight?	*Turn head to look around for fish.*
Shark eats three fish.	*Hold up three fingers.*
Mmm, what a delight!	*Shake head "yes."*
Shark eats four fish.	*Hold up four fingers.*
Yum, yum, yummy!	*Pretend to eat with both hands.*
Shark eats five fish.	*Hold up five fingers.*
That's a full tummy!	*Pat tummy.*

49

by Blake

Watch Out, Fish!

He's out there—lurking, swimming, searching for his next meal. Have your students create these booklets and turn a shark's hunt for fish into counting, fine-motor, and prereading practice. To prepare, reproduce the booklet on pages 53–55 for each child. Then read through the following directions and gather the appropriate materials. Assist your little ones in completing each booklet page before cutting the pages apart and stapling them in the correct sequence. To modify this activity for older students, mask out the numerals on each page before duplicating. Then direct students to write in a different number or color word on each page and illustrate accordingly. Youngsters will enjoy reading about this fishy feast with their families.

Cover: Color the shark. Write your name in the space provided.

Page 1: Sponge-print one fish shape below the shark.

Page 2: Glue two construction-paper fish shapes below the shark.

Page 3: Stencil three fish shapes to the right of the shark.

Page 4: Use a crayon to draw four fish shapes below the shark.

Page 5: Put five small fish stickers to the left of the shark.

Measuring Up To Sharks

Chances are, most of your youngsters have never seen a real shark. Use this activity to help your children discover how they measure up to sharks. Trace the large shark pattern from page 52 onto a clear transparency. Use an overhead or opaque projector to enlarge the shark image onto a 12-foot length of bulletin-board paper so that the length of the shark is approximately ten feet (the average length of a tiger shark). Use a marker to trace the outline onto the bulletin-board paper. Lay the shark outline on the floor and invite your students to compare the size of their bodies, hands, and feet to this fabulously large fish. For added fun, use tape to make a four-foot line on the floor to represent the smaller leopard shark's length; then make a 50-foot tape line to represent the length of the gigantic whale shark. Compare how many children it takes, lying head to toe, to equal each shark's length.

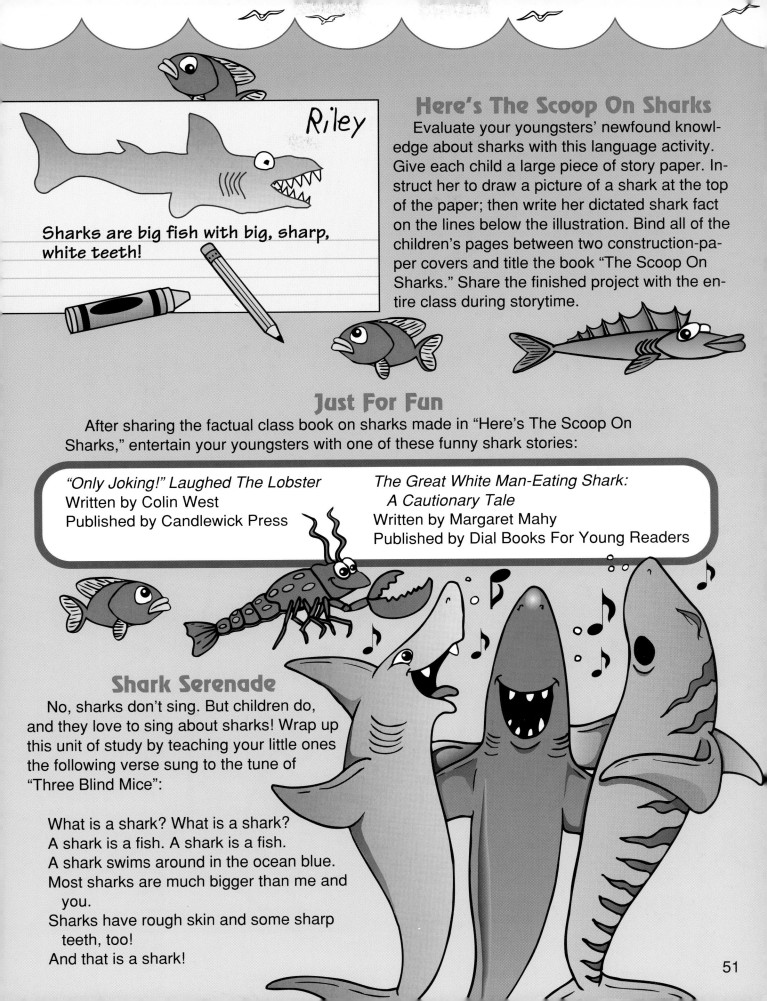

Riley

Sharks are big fish with big, sharp, white teeth!

Here's The Scoop On Sharks

Evaluate your youngsters' newfound knowledge about sharks with this language activity. Give each child a large piece of story paper. Instruct her to draw a picture of a shark at the top of the paper; then write her dictated shark fact on the lines below the illustration. Bind all of the children's pages between two construction-paper covers and title the book "The Scoop On Sharks." Share the finished project with the entire class during storytime.

Just For Fun

After sharing the factual class book on sharks made in "Here's The Scoop On Sharks," entertain your youngsters with one of these funny shark stories:

"Only Joking!" Laughed The Lobster
Written by Colin West
Published by Candlewick Press

The Great White Man-Eating Shark:
*   A Cautionary Tale*
Written by Margaret Mahy
Published by Dial Books For Young Readers

Shark Serenade

No, sharks don't sing. But children do, and they love to sing about sharks! Wrap up this unit of study by teaching your little ones the following verse sung to the tune of "Three Blind Mice":

What is a shark? What is a shark?
A shark is a fish. A shark is a fish.
A shark swims around in the ocean blue.
Most sharks are much bigger than me and
    you.
Sharks have rough skin and some sharp
    teeth, too!
And that is a shark!

Shark Patterns
Use with "Shark Smarts" on page 46, "A Sea Of Skills" on page 47, "Opposite Attack!" on page 48, and "Measuring Up To Sharks" on page 50.

©1997 The Education Center, Inc. • *JUNE* • TEC756

Watch Out, Fish!

by _____

©1997 The Education Center, Inc. • *JUNE* • TEC756

Shark sees **1** fish.

1

Shark sees **2** fish.

2

Shark sees **3** fish.

3

Shark sees **4** fish.

4

Shark eats **5** fish! Chomp!

5

Cool As Can Be At The Library

Introduce your students to the public library with Kool Kat, a furry feline who knows that the library is a cool place to be. Kool Kat will take your youngsters on a cat walk through activities that will help them discover that the library is the "purr-fect" way to spend a summer day!

ideas contributed by Lisa Leonardi

Meet Kool Kat

Set the stage for library learning by having Kool Kat visit your classroom. To prepare, use fabric paints to write the words "Cool As Can Be At The Library" on a T-shirt and allow the paint to dry. On the first day of your unit, arrange to have an assistant or adult volunteer available to supervise your class. Then dress up as Kool Kat. Wear the painted T-shirt, a pair of sunglasses, and a baseball hat. Next use face paints to paint whiskers and a catlike nose on your face.

Introduce yourself to your students as Kool Kat, the ultracool cat who knows where the fun is at—the library. Show youngsters some items that can be borrowed from the library, such as books, games, and videotapes. Then explain that any child may borrow these items from the library if she has a library card. Have Kool Kat read aloud a favorite book to the class, then teach students the following rap song. Meow! Now that's coooooooool!

Library Rap

Kool Kat knows the library is a fun place to be. Students will know it, too, after rapping the following chant. Beef up the beat by providing your little rap stars with some rhythm instruments. Boom-baboom-boom-ba-ba-boom!

Take it from a cat who's as cool as can be;
The public library is the place to be.
Boom-baboom-boom-ba-ba-boom!

Tapes and videos and books galore;
At the library you won't be bored!
Boom-baboom-boom-ba-ba-boom!

Story hours, computers, and so much more;
Your imagination is bound to soar!
Boom-baboom-boom-ba-ba-boom!

Kool Kat says, "If you want to have fun,
The public library is number one!"
Boom-baboom-boom-ba-ba-boom!

A Friend To You And Me

Help your little ones become acquainted with the workings of a library by inviting a librarian to visit your classroom. Create some excitement by writing a note on the chalkboard from Kool Kat telling youngsters that a very special friend will be visiting. Have the librarian tell students about the public library's summer program, story hours, upcoming events, and how students can get their own library cards. Invite her to read aloud a book about the library, such as *Check It Out!: The Book About Libraries* by Gail Gibbons (Harcourt Brace & Company). At the end of her visit, have her distribute a copy of the Kool Kat Library Klub award (page 60) to each child, to remind him that the library is a happening place to be!

Dear Boys and Girls,
   Today is a very special day.
   A classroom visitor is coming your way.
   Do you know who she might be?
   I'll give you clues—but only three:
      —She likes to help people.
      —She knows a lot about books.
      —She reads stories to children.
         Love,
         Kool Kat

Library Rules

1. Quiet please.
2. Treat books like friends.
3. Return books to the librarian.

Library Manners

Shhhh—quiet please. Help your youngsters understand the importance of library manners by reading aloud the book *The Library Dragon* by Carmen Agra Deedy (Peachtree Publishers, Ltd.). Then brainstorm with your little ones a list of library rules that are appropriate for the public library and for your classroom library, such as using a quiet voice, treating books with care, and returning books to their proper places. Write all the rules on a sheet of chart paper; then post the chart near your classroom library. As a child visits the classroom library, remind him to mind his manners please!

Kool Kat Bookbags

Get ready for the fabulous field trip to the library in "Look At Me At The Library" by making these bodacious bookbags. In advance, ask each parent to send in an old pillowcase for her child. Make a paw stamp by cutting one large circle and four smaller circles from a sponge. Hot-glue the circles to a square of heavy cardboard so that it resembles a pawprint. Next pour black fabric paint onto a paper plate. Have a child dip the paw stamp into the fabric paint (be sure to have each youngster wear an apron to prevent permanent stains on his clothing); then have him press the stamp onto his pillowcase. Encourage the child to continue in the same manner, making as many pawprints as he desires on his pillowcase. Allow the fabric paint to dry completely. Your little library patrons will love to tote these bookbags with them on your trip to the library.

Lisa

I liked the book about kittens.

Kool Kat Shelf Markers

Returning books to their proper places is easy with these Kool Kat shelf markers. Have each child use a brown marker to color the handle end on one side of a paint stick (available at your local hardware store). Next have him glue a precut felt baseball cap and a precut felt sunglasses shape to the top of the handle as shown. Instruct him to use a black marker to color in the sunglass lenses, then draw a nose and mouth. Assist him in gluing on bits of brown pipe cleaners to resemble whiskers; then twist a six-inch piece of brown pipe cleaner around the stick just below the handle to resemble a tail. Encourage students to use these markers on your field trip to the library to help mark the places where books were taken from the shelves. What a cool way to put books away!

Look At Me At The Library

Gear up for some firsthand library learning by taking your little ones on a field trip to your local public library. In advance, contact the children's librarian at your local public library to plan a tour of the library and a storytime. Then create some excitement by writing a note from Kool Kat on the chalkboard informing students of the trip and all the cool books they will have an opportunity to read. On the day of the trip, head to the library with bookbags (see "Kool Kat Bookbags") and shelf markers (see "Kool Kat Shelf Markers") in hand. During your visit, take a photo of each child exploring the library. Then, when you return to the classroom, make a class book about your visit. Invite each child to dictate what she most enjoyed about the library. Write her dictation at the bottom of a piece of paper labeled with her name. When the film has been developed, glue her photo on the page above her dictation. Bind the pages between construction-paper covers and title the book "Look At Me At The Library."

Sarah's
Kool Kat
Library Card

June 11, 1998

Mom, Dad, And Me At The Library

The library is not just for kids! Parents can enjoy the library too! The library can be a special place for families to share a love for books. Use copies of the parent letter on page 60 to suggest ways parents can help their children get excited about going to the library.

A Classroom Library

Your little librarians will be ready to read when you set up a play library in your classroom. Place a small desk and chair in the library area of your classroom. Stock the desk with a date stamp, pencils, pens, and a few Kool Kat shelf markers (see "Kool Kat Shelf Markers" on page 58). Place a small wagon next to the desk to hold returned books. Your youngsters will need library cards to visit this center, so reproduce and cut out a class supply of the Kool Kat Library Card on page 60. Glue each library card to a 3" x 5" index card. Distribute the cards to your students and have each child color Kool Kat.

To visit the center, a child shows his library card to the "librarian," who then stamps the back of the card using the date stamp. When the child is ready to leave the center, encourage him to place the books he read in the wagon. At the end of center time, help students replace the books on the shelves. Now that's a learning center your little ones will love to check out!

Check This Out!

Your little library patrons are sure to be spending lots of time in your library center with the addition of these books.

Red Light, Green Light, Mama And Me
Written by Cari Best
Published by Orchard Books

I Took My Frog To The Library
Written by Eric A. Kimmel
Published by Puffin Books

The Library
Written by Sarah Stewart
Published by Farrar, Straus, & Giroux, Inc.

Parent Letter
Use with "Mom, Dad, And Me At The Library" on page 59.

Dear Family,
   Our class is learning what a fun place the library can be! Here are some ways you and your child can beat the summer heat and "chill" together at the library.

- Get a library card.
- Mark a date on your calendar to visit the library together.
- Check out books about a topic your child would like to learn more about.
- Sign up your child for a story hour.
- Invite one of your child's friends to go along with your child to the library.

Happy reading!

_____
(Teacher)

Kool Kat Library Klub Award
Use with "A Friend To You And Me" on page 57.

_____
is an official member
of the
Kool Kat Library Klub!

Kool Kat Library Card
Use with "A Classroom Library" on page 59.

_____'s
Kool Kat
Library Card

Summer Nights

Can you see the flash of fireflies and hear the chirping of crickets? That's because summer nights are here, with all their delights for young and old alike. Use the activities on these pages to help little ones explore the things that make the long, hot evenings of summer so unique and so enjoyable.

ideas contributed by Lucia Kemp Henry

"Sense-ational" Summer Nights

Warm summer nights offer treats for all the senses! Share this poem with your youngsters; then help them make a list of the sights, sounds, tastes, smells, and feelings they associate with summer evenings.

On Summer Nights

On summer nights
I love to hear
Crickets chirp-chirp-chirping cheer.

On summer nights
I love to see
Fireflies flashing close to me.

On summer nights
I love to eat
Ice cream—melting, creamy, sweet.

On summer nights
I love to sniff
Flower smells; just take a whiff.

On summer nights
I love to feel
Warm breeze on me, head to heel.

On summer nights
I hear and touch,
See and smell and taste so much!

Hear
crickets
rain
frogs

See
fireflies
stars
fireworks

Taste
watermelon
hot dogs
lemonade

Smell
cut grass
flowers
food on grill

Feel
breeze
heat
grass

Summer Sunsets

Ever wonder why summer sunsets seem so brilliant? At sunset, the sun's rays are shining through the lower part of earth's atmosphere, where the dust, pollen, and pollutants scatter the light so that only the red and yellow wavelengths are visible to our eyes. In summer, there is more pollen in the air—intensifying the colors of the sunset.

Ask your little ones if they have seen a sunset lately. Help them describe a sunset's colors and position in the sky. Then involve them in producing their own artistic interpretations of a summer sunset. For each child, use a sponge to wet a large sheet of fingerpaint paper. Then apply one streak each of red, yellow, and orange fingerpaint to each child's paper. Invite the children to blend the three paint colors to create beautiful sunset paintings. Once the paintings have dried, send them home so that youngsters can share them with their families and compare their renderings to a *real* summer sunset.

A Roomful Of Fireflies

As night falls, the summer sky is filled with flashing fireflies. Share the book *Fireflies For Nathan* by Shulamith Levey Oppenheim (Tambourine Books) for a story that really sets the mood of a summer evening. Then invite little ones to create this firefly craft and bring that mood right into your classroom.

For each child, insert a thick pipe cleaner into a small Styrofoam® ball. Bend the free end of the pipe cleaner into a hook. Provide a container of fluorescent yellow tempera paint mixed with iridescent glitter. Ask each child to hold her pipe cleaner and dip the Styrofoam® ball into the paint; then hang it by the hook to dry. When the paint is dry, poke one small wing shape cut from tagboard into each side of the ball. Then dim the lights, play a recording of soft instrumental music, and invite little ones to make their fireflies dance through the air. It must be summer!

Shining Stars

There's nothing like being outside on a summer night to observe the twinkling stars. Capture that experience with this starry-night art project. To prepare, duplicate page 65 on white construction paper for each child. Have an adult volunteer or assistant help you cut out the circle as indicated on each sheet. Then photocopy each child's school photo. Tape a photocopy behind each sheet, so that the child's face shows through the opening.

Provide each child with her personalized sheet, crayons, fluorescent yellow tempera paint mixed with iridescent glitter, and some sponges cut into small star shapes. Invite her to color the tent, grass, and night sky, and then sponge-paint stars all over the sky. When the paint is dry, display the finished pictures on a bulletin board with the title "We're All Aglow Over Summer!" Be sure to pull the shades and dim the lights to fully appreciate the work of your shining stars!

Summer Supper Graph

Nothing says summer like a picnic supper outdoors on a warm evening. Prepare a graph to spark a discussion about your little ones' favorite foods for the great outdoors. Cut a long length of bulletin-board paper and draw lines to create several columns. Post the open graph near your circle area (within youngsters' reach); then engage students in a discussion of summer picnic foods. Have the class make a list, including main dishes, salads, and desserts. Then label the columns of your graph with some of the responses, and draw a picture of each food to cue nonreaders. Give each child a sticky note. Ask him to write his name on his note, then come up to the graph and place it in the column below his favorite summer picnic food. Discuss the results of the graph, emphasizing the concepts of *more, fewer,* and *equal.*

ice cream	hotdogs	pickles	potato salad	fried chicken	watermelon
Molly	Sam	Pete	Patty	Scott	Alex
Andrew	Tia			Matt	Janie
Carly				Chris	
				Julie	

And After Supper...

Long daylight hours mean that children are often allowed to stay up a little later and play outside a little longer in the summer. Teach youngsters some cooperative games perfect for summer evenings. Encourage them to teach these games to their families and neighborhood playmates.

For a game of Flock To The Nest, begin by spreading out a large picnic blanket in the center of a grassy area. Inform youngsters that this is the nest, and they are all birds. Instruct them to "fly" away into the grassy area. At your signal, have all the birds flock together into the nest (onto the blanket). For the next round, fold the blanket in half. Have your little birds again "fly" away, then return to the nest on your signal, cooperating so that everyone can find space on the blanket. Continue with a third round, folding the blanket in half once again.

For a game of Frog In A Pond, you'll need a picnic blanket and a beach ball (or other lightweight ball). Spread the picnic blanket on the ground, and explain that this is the pond. Place the ball in the center of the blanket and tell youngsters this is the frog. The object of the game is for all the children to hold the edges of the pond (the blanket) and help the frog (ball) "jump" in and out of the water. Have youngsters manipulate the blanket as they would a playground parachute, pulling it taut to make the ball "jump" and allowing slack to make the ball land. Once youngsters have the hang of it, add more beach-ball frogs to keep the game hoppin'!

A Summer Night Simulation

Set the stage for a midsummer night's fun right inside your classroom! Gather a few items that will help you set the mood, and ask parents to provide some simple finger foods for a summer evening menu. Ask an assistant or adult volunteer to help serve the food. After everyone has eaten, encourage youngsters to relax and gaze at the stars and firefly lights while you read a favorite story by lantern light.

To set the mood:
- Hang small, white blinking Christmas lights to serve as flashing fireflies.
- Affix some glow-in-the-dark stars to your classroom ceiling.
- Set one or two child-safe fans on a low setting to provide a simulated summer breeze.
- Play a recording of nature sounds to fill the air with the chirps of crickets and the peeps of frogs.
- Push tables and chairs out of the way, and spread picnic blankets on the floor.
- Turn off overhead lights, close the blinds, and switch on one or two battery-operated lights or lanterns.

A Midsummer Night's Menu

Vienna Sausages

Watermelon Wedges

Ice-Cream Cones

Single-Serving Juice Boxes

The Real Thing

If little ones enjoy your summer evening simulation, consider planning a *real* summer evening celebration. Invite parents to bring their children to an evening get-together at your school or a nearby park. Bring a grill and serve hot dogs, watermelon, and ice cream. Invite parents to join the children in playing the cooperative games described in "And After Supper..." on page 63. Provide jars for firefly-catching and hope for a spectacular sunset!

Cut out.

Note To The Teacher: Use with "Shining Stars" on page 62.

65

A-Camping We Will Go!

Load up your backpack, strap on your hiking boots, and grab your trail mix for a fun-filled cross-curricular camping excursion. Set up camp; then set out for some trailblazing learning adventures with your youngsters. Time to get packing!

ideas contributed by Suzanne Moore and Mackie Rhodes

Camp Talk

Get youngsters geared up for your camping adventure by reading one or two of the books listed in "Packed With Pleasure." After storytime, encourage students to recall what they learned about camping. Can they name some similarities and differences between camping and their daily home experiences? Ask students if they have ever been camping. Invite each camp-seasoned child to tell the class about her camping adventures. Then ask her to evaluate her trip. Did she enjoy it? Would she go again? Why or why not? Conclude by taking an oral head count of students who would like to go camping.

Just For The Fun Of It!

When early American pioneers traveled, they camped out of necessity. Today most people camp for the fun of it! They might camp under the stars, in tents, or in recreational vehicles. Some might travel by car, while others hike or canoe to their campsites. While camping, people participate in a variety of activities such as fishing, hiking, swimming, or sight-seeing. Invite students to share their families' outdoor adventures with this activity. Duplicate a class set of the parent letter on page 74. Have each child glue her letter to a 6" x 9" manila envelope. Encourage her to have her family enclose pictures of their camp or outdoor experiences in the envelope. After youngsters return their envelopes, display the pictures with the title "Camping—Just For The Fun Of It!"

Packed With Pleasure

Three Days On A River In A Red Canoe
Written by Vera B. Williams
Published by Greenwillow Books

Rusty's Red Vacation
Written by Kelly Asbury
Published by Henry Holt And Company, Inc.

Camping In The Temple Of The Sun
Written by Deborah Gould
Published by Bradbury Press

When I Go Camping With Grandma
Written by Marion Dane Bauer
Published by BridgeWater Books

When Daddy Took Us Camping
Written by Julie Brillhart
Published by Albert Whitman & Company

Bailey Goes Camping
Written by Kevin Henkes
Published by Greenwillow Books

Parent Letter

Ben Jackson

Let's Get Packing!

Now that students have some idea of what camping is about, try these activities to sharpen their reasoning and problem-solving skills.

Before embarking on any camping adventure, it's important to know what items to take along. To prepare for this activity, collect items that you might actually take on a camping excursion—such as a tent, sleeping bag, backpack, food, cooler, cooking utensils, sports equipment, and tools. Then ask youngsters to brainstorm a list of things needed for camping. Write student responses on a sheet of chart paper; then show them the real items. Ask them to name each item, then tell what its use might be. After youngsters discuss the camping items, invite them to take this challenge. Have small groups of students sort the items according to their uses—such as food, tools, or play equipment. How many categories can the group make?

Explain to students that campers fill backpacks with items needed for a camping hike or a daylong excursion. Then give each child a large sheet of construction paper with rounded corners at one end. Instruct her to fold the paper into thirds, with the rounded end overlapping the other end to resemble a backpack flap. Have her glue magazine cutouts (or her own drawings) of backpack items onto her unfolded paper, then write/dictate the name of each item. Label the pack with "What's In [child's name's] Backpack?" Then have the child decorate her folded pack to resemble a real backpack. Encourage her to tell a partner about the contents.

Now that everything is gathered for the camping trip, prepare students for the biggest challenge of all—packing everything to fit in the space available! To prepare, label three separate medium-sized boxes with "Car trunk," "Backpack," and "Cooler." Have student groups, in turn, pack each camping item in an appropriate box.

Going Camping

Prepare youngsters for an imaginary camping trip with this fun tune.

(sung to the tune of "I'm A Little Teapot")

I am going camping.	*Point thumbs proudly to chest.*
Time to pack	*Point to wristwatch.*
My tent, my bedroll,	*Make tent with hands; then fold hands to cheek.*
And a snack.	*Pretend to eat.*
I'll sit by the campfire—	*Warm hands over fire.*
Its glow so bright.	*Fan and wiggle fingers to resemble fire.*
Then snooze in my tent	*Pretend to snore.*
'Til the morning light!	*Open eyes wide, forming sun over head.*

Setting Up Camp

So you're all packed and ready to camp. The next step is to find your campsite and set up. With the following activities, youngsters will experience the realities of setting up house and housekeeping in the great outdoors.

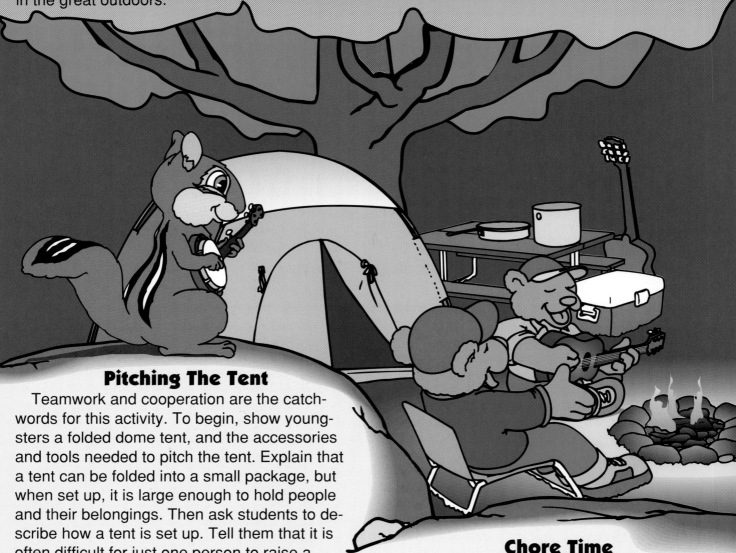

Pitching The Tent

Teamwork and cooperation are the catchwords for this activity. To begin, show youngsters a folded dome tent, and the accessories and tools needed to pitch the tent. Explain that a tent can be folded into a small package, but when set up, it is large enough to hold people and their belongings. Then ask students to describe how a tent is set up. Tell them that it is often difficult for just one person to raise a tent—it takes two or more people, and a lot of cooperation and communication. Afterward enlist volunteers to help you set up the dome tent in your dramatic play area. (If you don't have a tent, have youngsters help drape a large sheet over a table or chairs to represent a tent.)

Although your tent may be set up indoors, be sure to give students some hammering opportunities so they can experience what it's like to anchor the tent with pegs. To simulate this experience, invite youngsters to practice pounding tent pegs into Styrofoam® blocks. If desired, provide different objects with which children can pound—such as hammers, rocks, or even pieces of hard wood.

Chore Time

After the tent is pitched, it's time to set up housekeeping. Ask youngsters to unpack the camp items, then place them around the campsite. Encourage your class to decide as a group where and how to arrange the "kitchen" area. After setting up housekeeping, explain that when camping, many of the conveniences of home are not available. Challenge youngsters to brainstorm ways in which simple household chores and activities—such as cooking, cleaning, and bathing—might be performed. Where will water for cleanup come from? How will they stay warm? What will they do for light at night? After your discussion, engage small groups of youngsters in some pretend camp play at your indoor campsite. Happy camping!

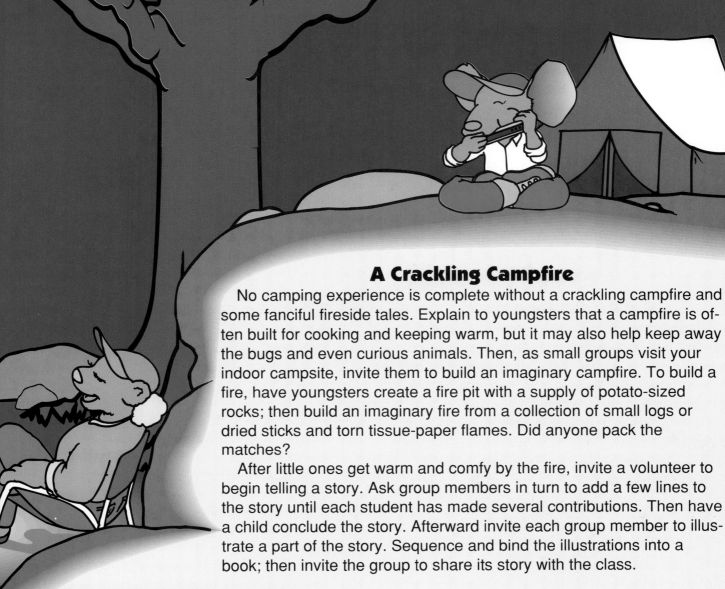

A Crackling Campfire

No camping experience is complete without a crackling campfire and some fanciful fireside tales. Explain to youngsters that a campfire is often built for cooking and keeping warm, but it may also help keep away the bugs and even curious animals. Then, as small groups visit your indoor campsite, invite them to build an imaginary campfire. To build a fire, have youngsters create a fire pit with a supply of potato-sized rocks; then build an imaginary fire from a collection of small logs or dried sticks and torn tissue-paper flames. Did anyone pack the matches?

After little ones get warm and comfy by the fire, invite a volunteer to begin telling a story. Ask group members in turn to add a few lines to the story until each student has made several contributions. Then have a child conclude the story. Afterward invite each group member to illustrate a part of the story. Sequence and bind the illustrations into a book; then invite the group to share its story with the class.

Sing Around The Campfire

It's a cool and cozy night by the campfire. The outdoor noises are humming and buzzing all around. A song swells in your throat as you absorb the contagious nighttime melodies. Well, go ahead—sing out! After all, singing 'round the campfire is a time-honored camping tradition that completes your outdoor experience. If you're at a loss for songs to sing, here's a list to get you started. Before long, youngsters will be requesting other old-time favorites and even making up their own tunes!

"On Top Of Old Smoky"
"I've Been Working On The Railroad"
"Oh, Suzannah"
"Clementine"
"She'll Be Coming 'Round The Mountain"
"Home On The Range"

Camp Courtesy

While camping may give one a carefree feeling, it's not an excuse to be careless. Teach youngsters to be careful, cautious, and courteous campers with these simple camping guidelines.

• Throw trash in appropriate containers.
• Be sure campfires are put out completely.
• Protect and respect wildlife.
• Respect the property and privacy of neighboring campers.
• Leave your campsite in the natural condition in which it was found—or better!

Outdoor Odyssey

A camping experience involves much more than setting up camp and building a campfire. Often hiking, fishing, swimming, and sight-seeing are associated with camping. Here are some ideas to help gear youngsters up for the most popular of these activities—a nature hike.

Bodacious Binoculars

Ready youngsters to focus on wildlife with these bodacious binoculars. To make a pair of binoculars, have a student tape two cardboard tubes together; then have him decorate his binoculars with a variety of craft items—such as stickers, buttons, feathers, and sequins. Tie the ends of a length of yarn through holes punched at one end of the binoculars to serve as the strap. What a view!

Energy Booster

Hiking can consume a lot of energy! Invite youngsters to help make this energy-boosting trail mix to pack for their cross-country trek. Then, when their fuel levels begin to drop, students will have a quick pick-me-up on hand.

Trail Mix

2 cups dry cereal rings
1 cup peanuts
1 cup coated chocolate candies
1 cup raisins
1 cup banana chips or shelled sunflower seeds

Mix all the ingredients in a large bowl. Scoop each serving into a separate zippered plastic bag labeled with a child's name. Makes six servings.

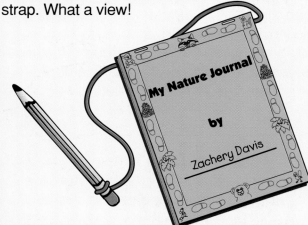

Nature Journal

Plan to fill in rest stops along your hike by encouraging youngsters to create nature journals. To make a journal for each child, duplicate the journal cover on page 75 on construction paper. Staple several sheets of paper between the front cover and a sheet of stiff cardboard (the back cover). Punch a hole in the top right corner of the cardboard book backing; then tie one end of a length of yarn through the hole. Tie the other end of the yarn around a pencil. Tell youngsters that whenever your class stops to rest on their nature hike, each child may illustrate something he observed along the way. After students return to the classroom, they may color their illustrations.

Hit The Trail

Time to hit the trail! Give each child a plastic grocery bag labeled with his name. Ask him to pack his nature journal and trail mix in the bag. If desired, also have him pack a small bottle of water. Then show him how to slip his arms into the bag handles so that the bag resembles a backpack. Have the child wear his binoculars around his neck. A-hiking we will go!

Camp Cuisine

The great outdoors can really work up a person's appetite, as well as present some interesting cooking challenges. Here are some ideas to help youngsters grasp the fun—and frustration—that comes along with camp cooking.

Solar-Cooked S'mores

The most natural cooking source comes directly from the sun up above—solar heat. When using a solar oven, the sun's energy is captured so that food can cook slowly in the natural heat. To make a solar oven, line a shoebox with aluminum foil, pressing the dull side of the foil against the box. Then, on a warm sunny day, invite each child to prepare the recipe shown. Have her put her snack in the solar oven; then place the oven in direct sunlight (preferably in the noonday sun) for approximately 30 minutes. When the chocolate has melted, the S'mores are ready to eat. Mmmm…youngsters will be asking for s'more!

S'Mores
(one serving)

2 graham crackers
1 miniature chocolate bar
2–4 miniature marshmallows

Sandwich the chocolate bar and marshmallows between the graham crackers; then wrap the treat in a piece of foil, shiny side out. Place in a solar oven as directed above.

Fireside Favorites

Hot dogs and marshmallows! These fireside favorites are must-haves for any camping adventure. To give youngsters the experience of cooking over the open hearth, provide each child with a wooden skewer and a few marshmallows or a precooked hot dog. Have him slip his choice of food onto the end of his skewer, then roast it over the imaginary class-made fire. Sizzle, sizzle, yum!

Lightweight Foods

Many campers—especially those who hike to their campsites—pack freeze-dried foods for their meals. These prepackaged foods are lightweight, need no refrigeration, and can be easily prepared. Give youngsters some firsthand experience in preparing and tasting freeze-dried food with this activity. Obtain a can of applesauce and a package of freeze-dried applesauce (check your local sporting goods store). Pour the contents of each into separate containers; then encourage youngsters to voice their observations. Afterward have students help prepare the freeze-dried applesauce according to package directions. Ask each child to sample each dish; then have her place a personalized apple cutout onto a two-column graph under her preference—the canned or freeze-dried variety. Compare the results. Which applesauce wins?

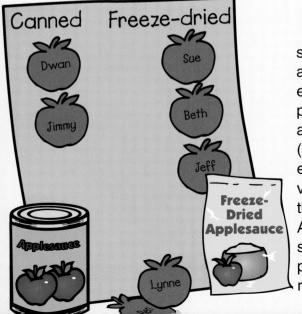

71

Nighttime At Camp

Darkness has blanketed the campsite and you wonder how to fill the time until bedtime. Try some of these fun nighttime camp activities to round out your youngsters' camping experiences.

Starry, Starry Night

Ooohh! The awesome starry night is a camping sight to behold! Obtain a chart of the night sky, or any other illustrations or photos of the constellations. Show these to your class, pointing out some of the constellations—such as the Big Dipper and Ursa Major. Explain that the constellations got their names from people who saw dot-to-dot outlines of things among the stars. Then invite youngsters to create their own constellations. Provide each small group of students with a length of black bulletin-board paper, star stickers, and white chalk. Have each group randomly stick stars on its paper, then make celestial creations by connecting the stars with chalk. Mount the constellations on or near the ceiling for students' stargazing pleasure at rest time.

Shadows In The Night

These shadowy tent capers will keep youngsters fascinated for hours! Set up a battery-operated lantern or flashlight inside the tent in your camping center (see "Pitching The Tent" on page 68); then dim the classroom lights. Invite a small group of youngsters to sit inside the tent. Have each child in turn create a shadow in the light of the lantern as the other students describe what they see. If desired, ask the students outside the tent to describe their observations also. Afterward ask each child to draw a shadow of something she might see while on a camping trip; then ask her to tell the class a short story about her illustration.

Lights Out!

Entice your young campers to bed down in their own cozy sleeping bags with this idea. To prepare, send each child home with a copy of the parent request letter on page 74. After each student brings his two towels to school, stack and tape his towels together along one short and one long edge to resemble a sleeping bag. Have the child roll up his sleeping bag and store it with his other belongings. Then, at rest time, invite youngsters to retrieve their bedrolls and curl up in them under the starry night sky (see "Starry, Starry Night"). Good night, all!

Break It Down

Setting up camp is a lot of work—but so is breaking down camp! The tent must be disassembled and refolded. The sleeping bags must be rolled tightly. All the kitchen items must be cleaned and repacked. Everything must be loaded back into the car. Campers must check and double-check to make sure the campfire is completely extinguished, all trash has been properly disposed of, and the campsite is left in its natural condition. To break down your classroom campsite, assign each small team of youngsters a different task. Encourage the teams to perform their tasks as efficiently and neatly as possible. After everything is packed and ready for the trip home, invite youngsters to give themselves three cheers for a job well done. Whew! It's a lot of work, but well worth the fun of camping!

More Books About Camping And The Great Outdoors

Do Not Disturb
Written by Nancy Tafuri
Published by Greenwillow Books

The Lost Lake
Written by Allen Say
Published by Houghton Mifflin
  Company

Where The River Begins
Written by Thomas Locker
Published by Dial Books

*Crinkleroot's Guide To Walking
  In Wild Places*
Written by Jim Arnosky
Published by Bradbury Press

Camping Is "Sense-ational"!

Help youngsters summarize their camping adventures with this "sense-ational" activity. To begin, ask youngsters to describe their actual or imaginary camping sensory experiences. Encourage them to consider all the senses—sight, sound, smell, taste, and touch. Write their responses on a sheet of chart paper; then invite each child to select one of the experiences to illustrate on a half-sheet of paper. Have her mount her drawing on a construction-paper tent cutout labeled with her name. Then ask her to write/dictate a sentence describing the sensory experience depicted by her illustration.

To display the illustrations, title a bulletin board "Camping is 'Sense-ational'!" Divide the board into five columns; then label each column for one of the five senses. Attach each child's illustration in the appropriate column. A starry night, chirping crickets, smoke in the air, and sweet, gooey, roasted marshmallows. Ahhh, yes, camping *is* sensational!

73

Parent Letter

Use with "Just For The Fun Of It!" on page 66.

Dear Parent,

Has your family ever been camping? Do you have photos of your camping adventure? If so, please share some of them with our class! Simply label the back of each photo with your child's name and a brief description of the picture. Enclose the pictures in the attached envelope; then return the envelope to school. The pictures will be used in a class display about camping. At the end of our unit, the photos will be returned to you. (If you do not have camping photos to send, help your child find and cut out magazine pictures of outdoor/nature activities.) Thanks for your help!

_____
(teacher)

Parent Request Letter

Use with "Lights Out!" on page 72.

Dear Parent,

We are learning all about camping. Did you know that America's pioneers camped as they explored our country?

During our rest time, we will be napping in bedrolls similar to those used by the pioneers. To do this, we need your help. Please send two same-sized bath towels to school with your child by _____. These will be taped together to
                                                                      (date)
be used as a sleeping bag for your child. We'll return them when we break down our classroom campsite.

Thank You!

_____
(teacher)

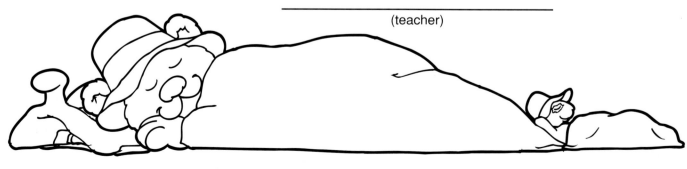

My Nature Journal

by

Wonderful Worms & Super Snails

Wiggle your way into the wonderful world of worms and snails with this multidisciplinary unit. Even if you're squeamish by nature, after doing these activities, you'll grow a soft heart for these soft-bodied, slippery creatures!

ideas contributed by Suzanne Moore and Mackie Rhodes

Soft, Slimy, And Super!

Slip right into this unit by sharing the following information about worms and snails with your class. If desired, share the books *Wonderful Worms* by Linda Glaser (The Millbrook Press) and *Snail* by Jens Olesen (Silver Burdett Company) with your class.

- A worm is sensitive to light. It prefers dark areas and the night.
- A worm has a soft, segmented body and no legs.
- A worm has no ears, but can feel sound vibrations with its body.
- A worm's mouth is at one end of its body.
- A worm breathes through its skin.

- A snail glides along a surface on its long, flat foot.
- A snail's head and mouth are on its foot.
- A snail's teeth are located *on* its tongue.
- A snail's eyes are on the tips of its tentacles. Its tentacles can retract into its head.
- The soft body of a snail is topped with a shell.
- The snail is born with the shell.

- Worms and snails are boneless animals.
- Worms and snails produce mucus, a slimy substance, to keep their skin moist and to help them move along smoothly.
- Worms and snails live in shady, moist environments.
- If a worm or snail is exposed to air too long, it may dry up and die.

A Slippery Safari

Now that youngsters know some interesting facts about these slimy outdoor animals, invite them on a safari to find some real live worms and snails. Equip each child with a digging tool—such as a craft stick or plastic spoon. Then guide youngsters to look for dark, damp areas to find these creatures. Areas under bushes, logs, rocks, or leaf piles are ideal locations in which to discover worms and snails. Have students transport their slimy finds to class in a container filled with moist soil and a few wet leaves.

If your school is not near a natural area, check with a local garden center to learn where you might be able to find or purchase worms and snails.

Observation Stations

Set up these temporary homes for your slippery critters and give youngsters the opportunity to observe the lifestyles of worms and snails. Set up the observation stations in a cool area of your classroom, out of direct sunlight. Stock the center(s) with books about worms and snails, as well as with hand lenses, craft sticks, and writing supplies. As youngsters observe these fascinating creatures, invite them to write about or illustrate their observations. After completing this unit, be sure to return the animals to their natural habitat.

The Worm Ward

Prepare for a "worm" welcome with this temporary worm home. To begin, fill the bottom of a fishbowl, aquarium, or large glass jar with gravel. Layer damp, loosely packed soil on top of the gravel. Ask your class to introduce the captured worms to their new home; then add worm food—such as dead leaves, coffee grounds, cornmeal, and healthful table scraps (foods like carrot peels and bits of fruit and vegetables). Keep the outside of the container covered with dark paper when youngsters are not using this observation station. Moisten the soil daily with a spray bottle, using rainwater if possible. Burrow on down and make yourselves at home, little wormies!

Snail Hotel

Create luxury accommodations for your slimy guests with this snail hotel. To prepare, fill the bottom of an aquarium with gravel; then add at least four inches of damp soil. (Keep the soil moist with a spray bottle filled with rainwater.) Put a few small plants—roots and all—in the aquarium to serve as a food source for the snails. Other snail foods that you might include are fresh green leaves and vegetable bits. To meet the calcium needs of the snails, sprinkle a mixture of crushed limestone and flour into the aquarium, also. Then, if desired, add moss, grass, sticks, and rocks to make the snail home more natural. To encourage egg laying, cover the lower half of the snail hotel with dark paper. Ask students to place the snails into their temporary home; then top the aquarium with a mesh or cardboard cover. Now your snail guests can slip into something comfortable—the snail hotel!

Touch Me, Please!

Although worms and snails are slimy, slippery creatures, they *are* touchable! Use this rhyme to help youngsters decide whether or not they have the will to actually touch one or both of these harmless animals. For each animal, create a two-columned chart titled "Would You Hold A [(Worm/Snail] In Your Hand?" Label one column with "Yes" and the other with "No." On each of two separate half-sheets of paper, have each child trace around his hand and write his name. Then place a worm and a snail on separate damp paper towels. Recite each verse of the rhyme below while showing students the corresponding animal (afterward return the animals to their homes). Ask each student to indicate his answer to each question in the rhyme by either drawing the animal inside his hand outline ("yes") or coloring the outline a solid flesh color ("no"). Attach each child's drawings under the appropriate columns on the charts. Compare the responses to determine how cautious or carefree your class feels about handling worms and snails. The results may be touching!

Would You Hold A Worm In Your Hand?

Yes

Donald

Katie

Stephanie

Kenny

No

Charles Glenda

Kim

Would You Hold It In Your Hand?

Wiggly, squiggly worms
In dirt are wonderfully grand.
But if you found one on the ground,
Would you hold it in your hand?

Slippery, slimy snails
In shells are wonderfully grand.
But if you found one on the ground,
Would you hold it in your hand?
　　　　　　　　—Suzanne Moore

Handle With Care

Whether they want to touch your slippery guests or not, youngsters are probably squirming with curiosity about worms and snails. Invite students to observe these interesting creatures up close and personal with this activity. To begin, moisten some paper towels; then place a few worms and snails on the towels for youngsters to observe. Periodically moisten the towels using a spray bottle. To prevent the animals from drying out, return them to their homes after a brief observation period. If additional observation time is desired, transfer a different set of animals to the paper towels. For an underside view of the animals, place them in a clear plastic container or a plastic bag. Encourage youngsters to examine the creatures, *gently* moving them about with their fingers or craft sticks. Record their comments and discoveries on corresponding worm or snail cutouts. Then display the cutouts in the center(s) created in "Observation Stations" on page 77.

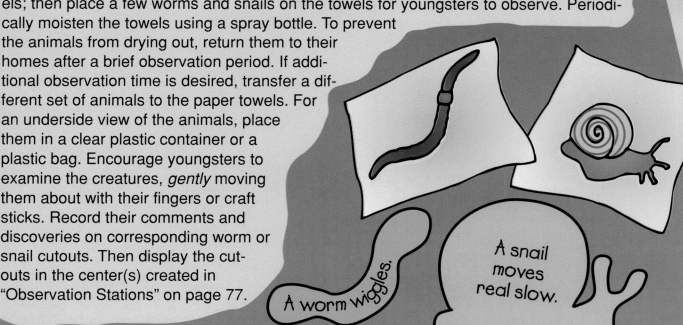

A worm wiggles.

A snail moves real slow.

78

Slide, Squiggle, Stretch, And Squirm

Worm some movement opportunities into your youngsters' day with this idea. Ask students to describe the movements of a worm and a snail. How are their movements alike? Different? If desired, observe each animal separately to examine its movement patterns. Then arrange a simple obstacle course in your classroom or gym to include a few different surface textures—such as a smooth tile floor, a bumpy carpet, and a soft gym mat. Invite students to negotiate the obstacle course, crawling like worms under, around, and through the different components. Then encourage them to repeat the course as they creep along like snails. Afterward have youngsters discuss their movement experiences. After all that stretching, squiggling, and sliding, youngsters just might understand why oozier is easier!

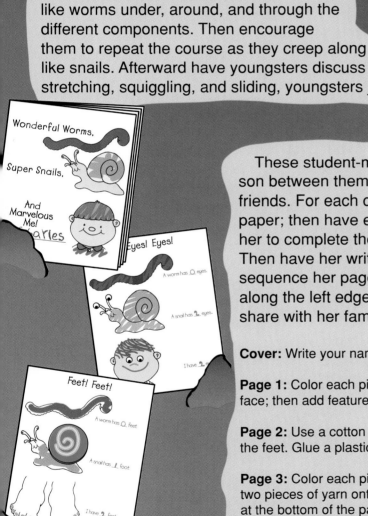

The Final Analysis

These student-made books will help youngsters make the comparison between themselves and their squiggly, slippery, soft-bodied friends. For each child duplicate pages 82–85 on white construction paper; then have each child cut out her book cover and pages. Invite her to complete the pages according to the provided suggestions. Then have her write the appropriate numeral in each blank. Have her sequence her pages behind the cover, then staple her book together along the left edge. Encourage the child to take her book home to share with her family.

Cover: Write your name on the line. Color the pictures.

Page 1: Color each picture. Glue wiggle eyes on the snail's tentacles and the child's face; then add features to the child's picture to resemble yourself.

Page 2: Use a cotton swab to paint the worm, the snail's body, and the toenails on the feet. Glue a plastic milk-jug lid onto the snail's body to represent its shell.

Page 3: Color each picture. Glue short pieces of yarn across the worm's body. Glue two pieces of yarn onto the snail's head to represent its tentacles. Trace your fingers at the bottom of the page.

Just The Facts!

For more information and activities on worms and snails, obtain copies of *Wormology* and *Snailology* by Michael Elsohn Ross (Carolrhoda Books, Inc.). These books give simple, but interesting facts about these animals, as well as activities that can be adapted to suit your students' interests and needs.

A Worm's World

Expand youngsters' knowledge about the wonderful world of worms with these ideas.

Burrow Bound

Earthworms live underground, forming burrows by pushing and pulling their bodies through the dirt. Entice your young worm enthusiasts to create models of a worm's home with this activity. For each child put a small amount of shaving cream and brown fingerpaint onto a tray or cookie sheet. Encourage the child to mix the two substances with his fingers, then create worm burrows in the mixture. Ask him to gently press a large sheet of construction paper over his design, then carefully lift the paper off to expose a worm burrow impression.

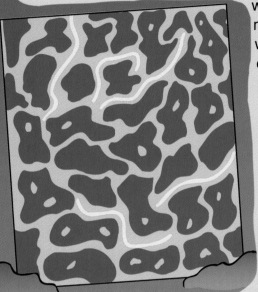

Set the impressions aside to dry while students engage in a bit more sensory play with the shaving-cream mixture.

After each child's impression dries, invite him to position a few cooked spaghetti worms along the burrows on his paper (the starch in a wet noodle will make it stick to the paper). Point out that as long as a worm's body is moist, it remains soft and pliable like a noodle. Ask youngsters what they think will happen to worms—and their noodles—if they get too dry. Then have youngsters check their papers periodically to see if they answered correctly.

Worms In Hiding

The pinkish brown color of earthworms helps them to blend into their natural surroundings so that their enemies—moles, birds, and other animals—cannot easily find them. Use this idea to help youngsters understand how *camouflage* helps a worm hide from its enemies. To prepare, rinse a supply of rubber fishing worms in a variety of colors and sizes. Record the number of worms representing each color on a notecard. Prior to taking your class outdoors, scatter the worms in a natural area of the school grounds. Then invite youngsters to pretend they are hungry, worm-eating animals in search of a meal. Challenge them to find as many worms as possible; then have each child tell how many worms of each color he found. Which color worms were hardest to find? Did the class find all the worms? If not, send them on a search for the missed worms. "Every worm come out of hiding, please!"

Stretch And Measure

Students will stretch their math skills when they measure worms in this activity. Invite each student pair to select a rubber worm to measure. Or, if desired, the partners might choose a live worm. Have the pair stretch the worm out as straight as possible, then measure it with a set of multilink cubes, paper clips, or other type of nonstandard unit of measure. Ask each set of partners to share its findings with another student pair to compare the lengths of the two different worms. Ready, stretch, measure!

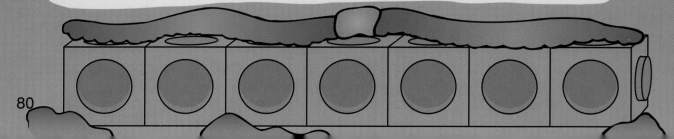

Snail-mania!

If your youngsters are fascinated with the gentle, lovable snail, they're sure to enjoy these snail-related activities.

What's Afoot?

Snails are—and they're leaving a trail of evidence to prove it! Share *Mr. Carey's Garden* by Jane Cutler (Houghton Mifflin Company) with your class; then invite youngsters to make their own snail trails. To begin, have each child trace her foot (with her shoe on) on a sheet of construction paper, and then cut out her foot outline. Next ask her to paint a yogurt-container lid with a mix-

ture of equal parts of glue and brown tempera paint. After the lid dries, help her glue a spiral of yarn inside the lid so that it resembles a snail's shell. Have the child glue the shell onto her foot cutout. Then ask the child to create a trail along a black sheet of construction paper using iridescent glitter glue or fabric paint. Finally, after the trail dries, have the child glue her snail onto her paper. Display the projects with the title "Snails Are Afoot!"

Jeepers, Creepers...

Where'd ya get those peepers? And that big foot? And that spiraled shell? Snails are certainly odd-looking creatures! But then, they are born with all that strange equipment. Here's an activity to help youngsters recall the more outstanding features of a snail. After cre-

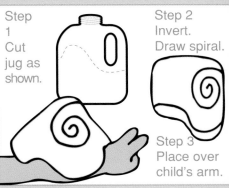

Step 1 Cut jug as shown.

Step 2 Invert. Draw spiral.

Step 3 Place over child's arm.

ating the snail shell (see the diagram), simply place it over a child's arm as shown; then encourage him to creep his snail-converted arm along the edge of the table as the class sings this song. Repeat the song, giving each child the opportunity to role-play the snail. So, where *did* ya get those eyes?

(sung to the tune of "Twinkle, Twinkle, Little Star")

Creeping, creeping, little snail.
Creeping in your little shell.
Your big foot slides on the ground.
Your tentacles look round and round.
Creeping, creeping, little snail.
Creeping in your little shell.

From Dough To Escargot

Youngsters might not enjoy eating the real thing, but these dough escargots just might hit the spot! To make one, give each child half a round of refrigerated sugar-cookie dough. Ask him to roll the dough into a rope, then coil it into a spiral, leaving one end slightly extended to represent the snail's head. Have him poke two broken pretzel sticks into the snail's head to represent tentacles. Bake the dough escargots at 350°F for 6–10 minutes. Then invite youngsters to enjoy the cooled treats. Yummy-o! Escargot!

Wonderful Worms,

Super Snails,

And Marvelous Me!

by _____

(Name)